WORSHIP FAVORITES FOR UKULEL

ISBN 978-1-5400-1336-1

7777 W. Bluemound Rd. P.O. Box 13819 Milwaukee, WI 53213

Visit Hal Leonard Online at
www.halleonard.com

At the Cross
(Love Ran Red)

Words and Music by Matt Redman, Jonas Myrin, Chris Tomlin, Ed Cash and Matt Armstrong

D
A
Em7
ren - der my life. I'm in awe of You, I'm in awe of You. Where Your
G
D
A
To Coda
love ran___ red and my sin washed white, I owe all to You, I owe
1.
Em7
G
D
Dsus4
D
all to You, Je - sus. 2. There's a
2.
Bridge
Em7
G
Bm
all to You. Here my hope is found, here on ho - ly ground.
D
A
G
Here I bow down, here I bow down. Here, arms o - pen wide,
Bm
Asus4
A
D.S. al Coda
here You saved my life._ Here I bow down, here I bow. At the
Coda
Em7
G
D
all to You, Je - sus.

Because He Lives, Amen

Words and Music by William J. Gaither, Gloria Gaither, Daniel Carson,
Chris Tomlin, Ed Cash, Matt Maher and Jason Ingram

D G C D Em D
lives. A - men! A - men! Let my
To Coda
1.
G D G C D Em C
song join the one that nev - er ends, be-cause He lives.
G Em C G
2. I was
2.
Bridge
D G Cmaj7 D
ends. Be-cause He lives, I can face to - mor - row. Be-cause He
G Cmaj7 D G Cmaj7
lives, ev - 'ry fear is gone. I know He holds my
Em D C
D.S. al Coda
life, my fu - ture in His hands. A -

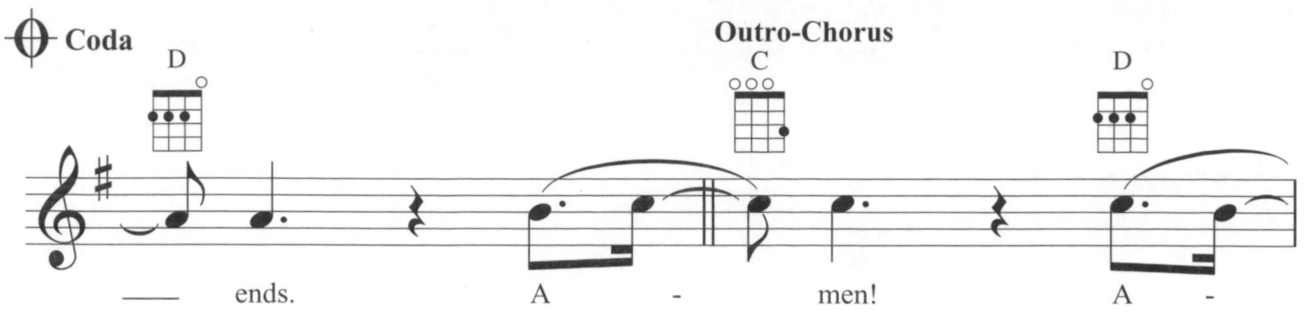
Coda
Outro-Chorus
D
C
D
ends. A - men! A -

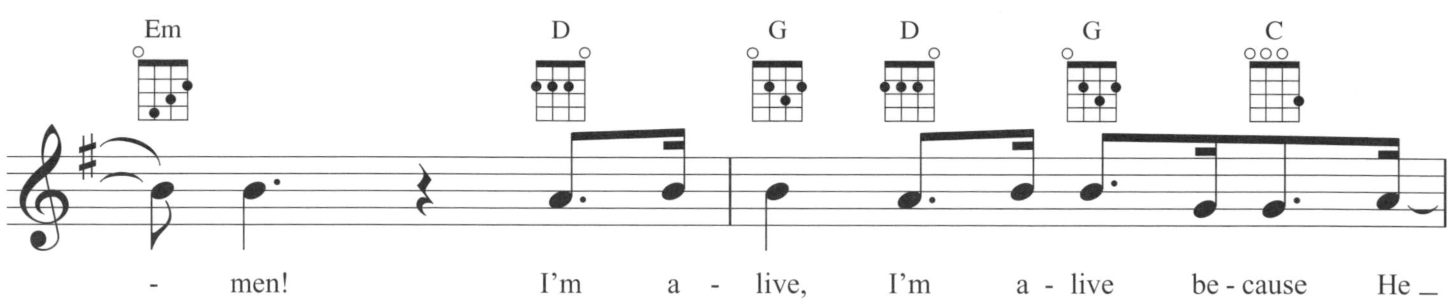
Em
D
G
D
G
C
- men! I'm a - live, I'm a - live be - cause He

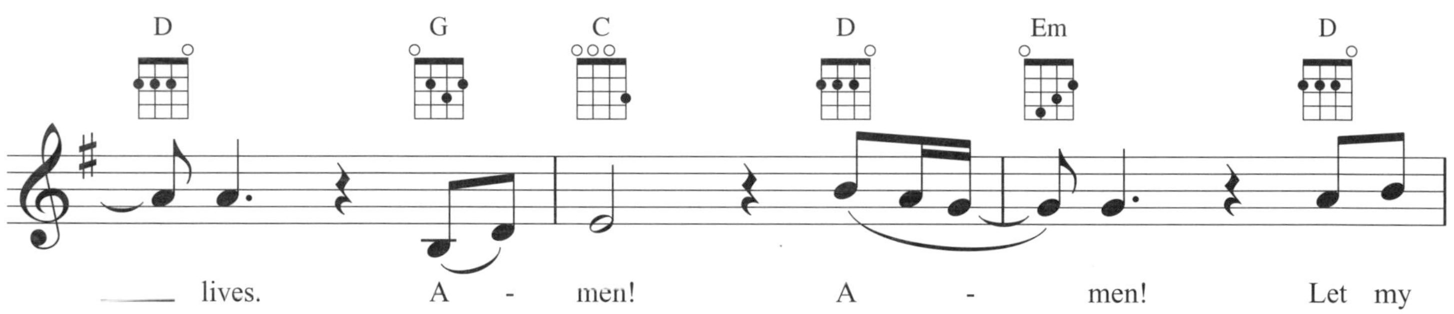
D
G
C
D
Em
D
lives. A - men! A - men! Let my

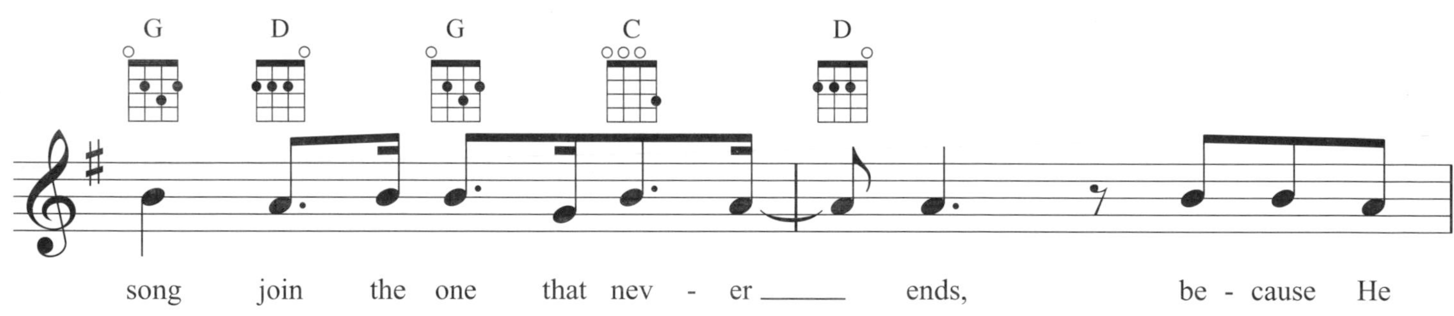
G
D
G
C
D
song join the one that nev - er ends, be - cause He

Em
C
G
Em
C
G
lives, be-cause He lives.

Days of Elijah

Words and Music by Robin Mark

G
C
G
D
we are the voice in the des - ert cry - ing, "Pre - pare ye the way of the Lord."
we are the la - bor-ers in Your vine-yard, de - clar - ing the Word of the Lord.
Chorus
Be - hold, He comes, rid-ing on the clouds, shin-ing like the sun
at the trum - pet call. Lift your voice; it's the year of Ju - bi - lee,
and out of Zi - on's hill sal - va - tion comes.
1.
2.
2. And
Bridge
There is no god like Je - ho - vah, there is no god like Je - ho - vah,

G
D
there is no god like Je - ho - vah, there is no god like Je - ho - vah.
G
C
There is no god like Je - ho - vah, there is no god like Je - ho - vah,
G
D
there is no god like Je - ho - vah, there is no god like Je - ho - vah.
Chorus
N.C.
G
C
Be - hold, He comes, rid - ing on the clouds, shin ing like the sun
G
D
G
at the trum - pet call. Lift your voice; it's the year of Ju - bi - lee,
1.
2.
C
G
D
G
G
and out of Zi-on's hill sal - va - tion comes. Be - hold, He comes.

Before the Throne of God Above

Words and Music by Vikki Cook and Charitie Bancroft

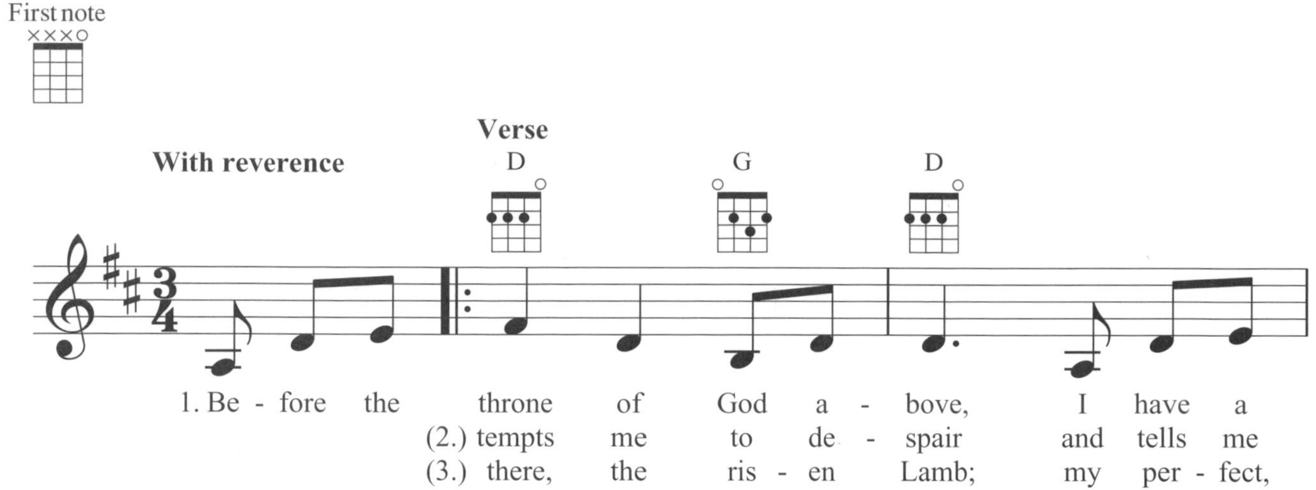

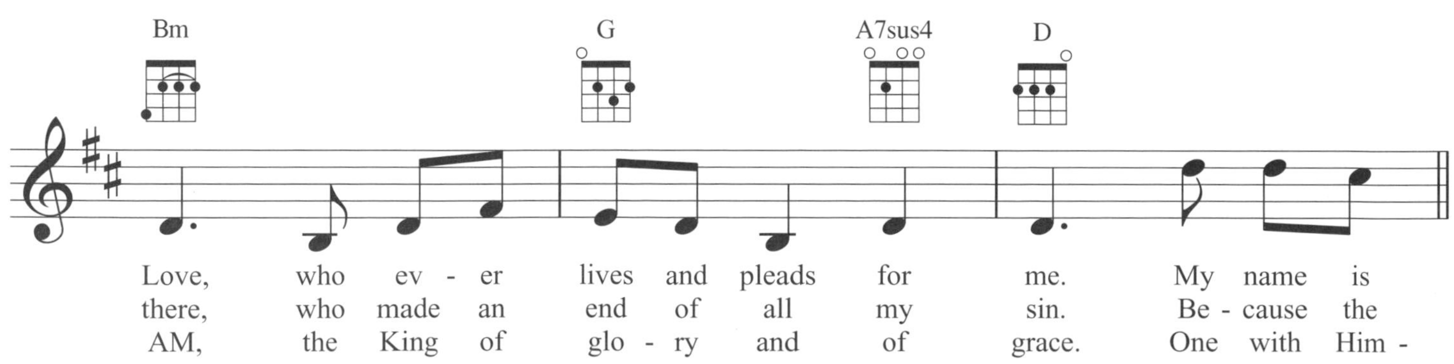

G D A G D
grav - en on His hands, my name is writ - ten on His
sin - less Sav - ior died, my sin - ful soul is count - ed
self, I can - not die. My soul is pur - chased by His

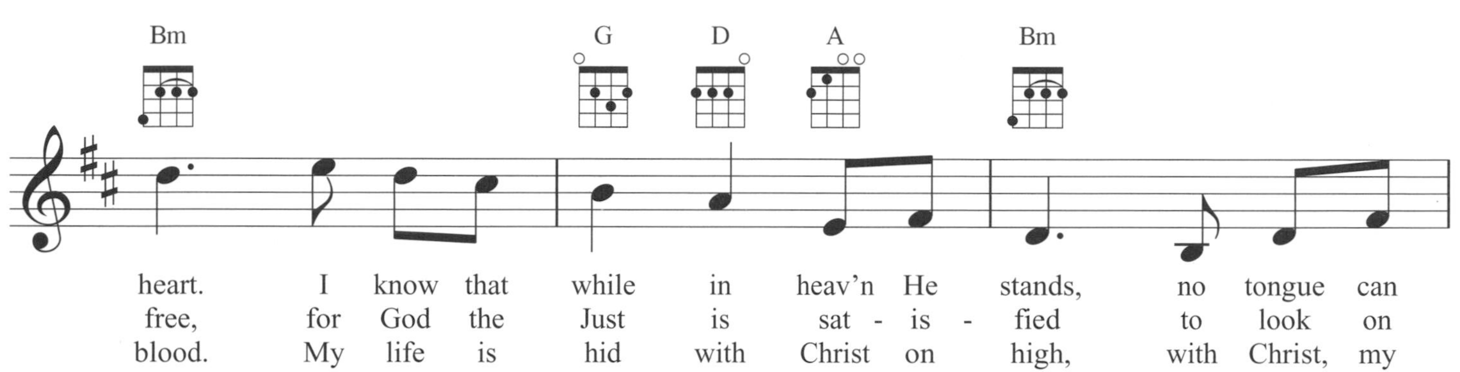
Bm G D A Bm
heart. I know that while in heav'n He stands, no tongue can
free, for God the Just is sat - is - fied to look on
blood. My life is hid with Christ on high, with Christ, my

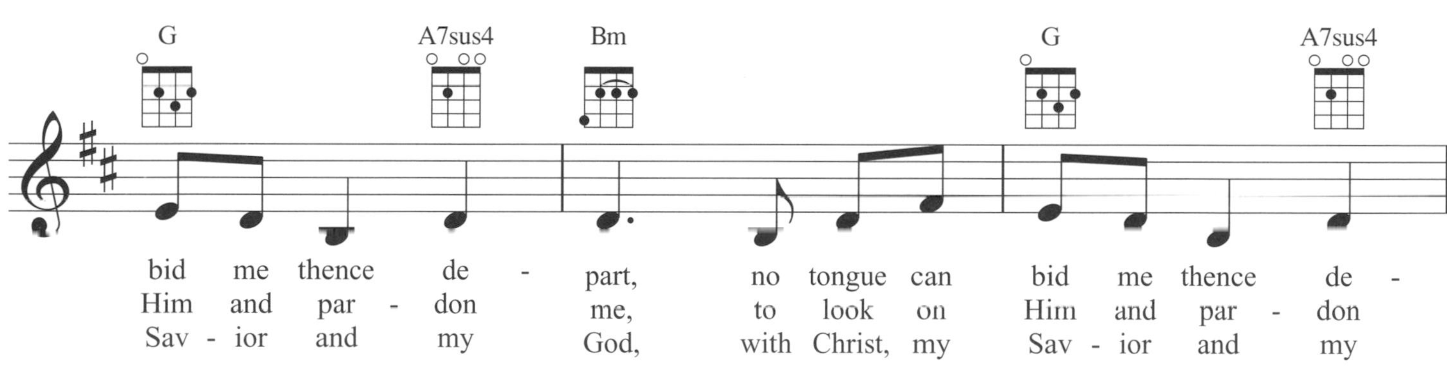
G A7sus4 Bm G A7sus4
bid me thence de - part, no tongue can bid me thence de -
Him and par - don me, to look on Him and par - don
Sav - ior and my God, with Christ, my Sav - ior and my

1., 2.
3.
D D
part. 2. When Sa - tan God.
me. 3. Be - hold Him

Build Your Kingdom Here

Words and Music by Rend Collective

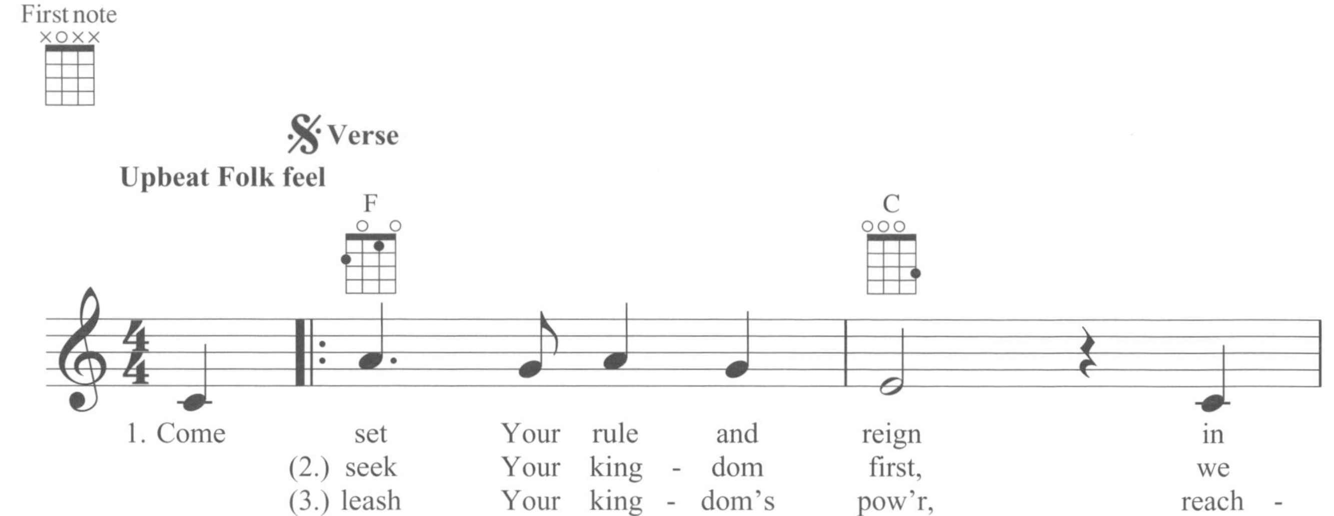

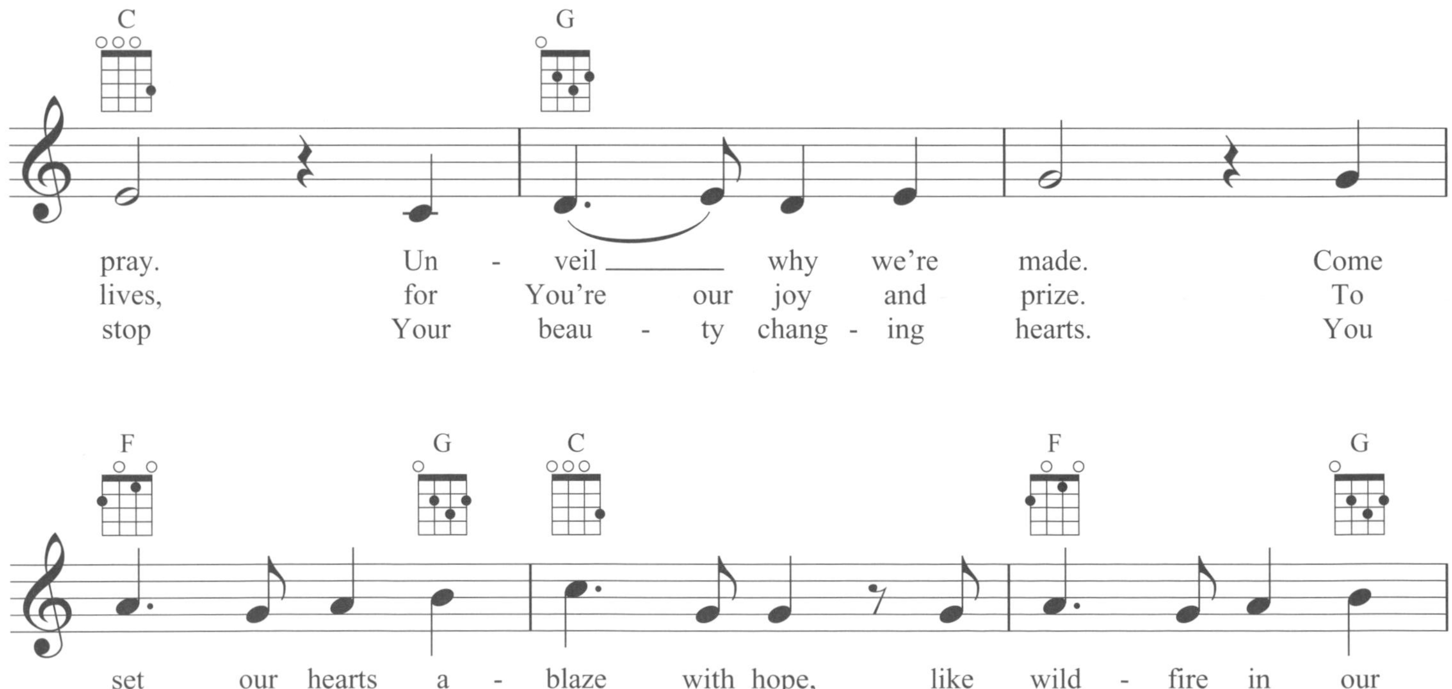

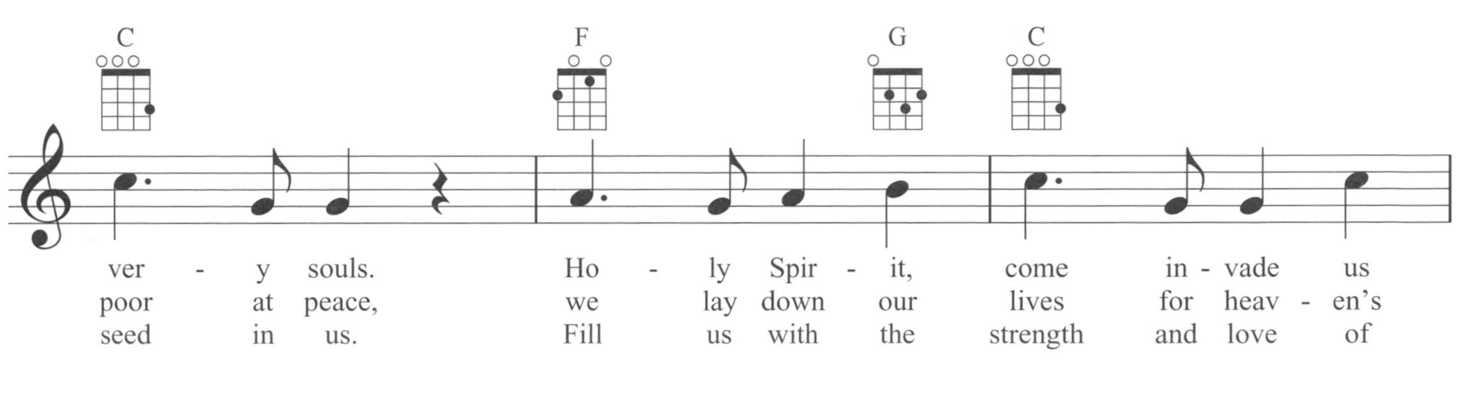
C F G C
ver - y souls. Ho - ly Spir - it, come in - vade us
poor at peace, we lay down our lives for heav - en's
seed in us. Fill us with the strength and love of

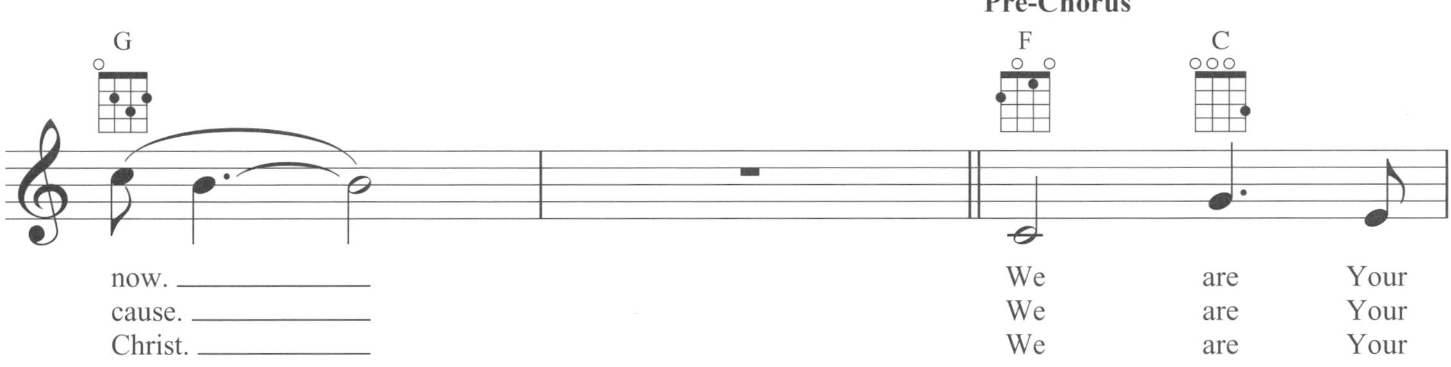
Pre-Chorus
G F C
now.
cause.
Christ.
We are Your
We are Your
We are Your

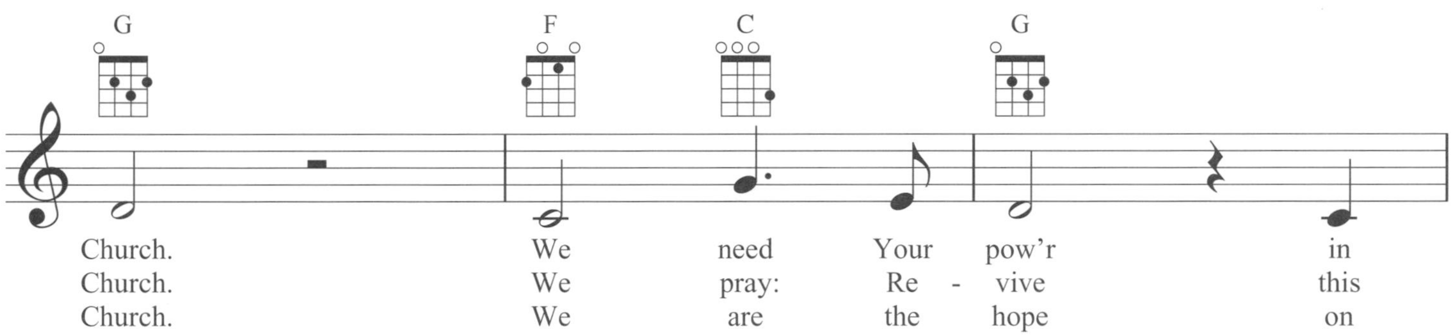
G F C G
Church. We need Your pow'r in
Church. We pray: Re - vive this
Church. We are the hope on

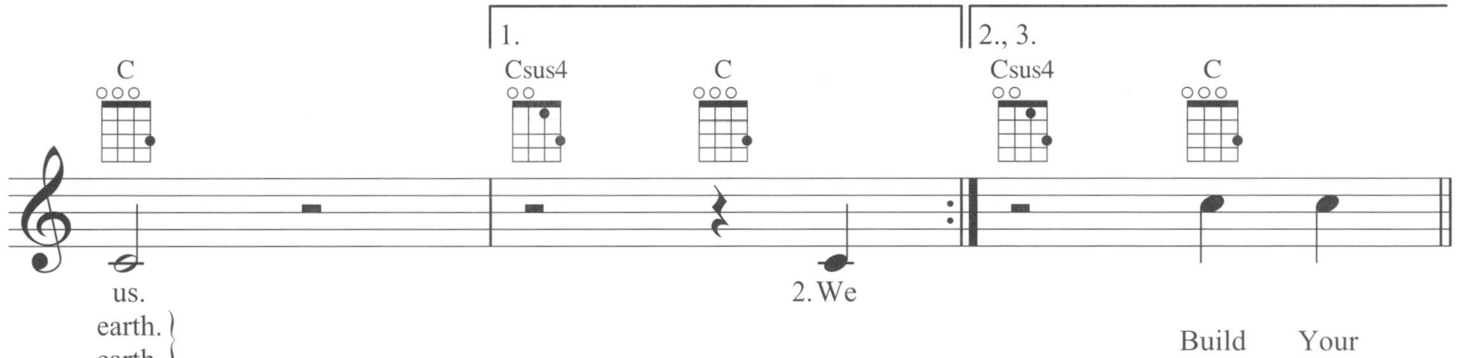
1.
2., 3.
C Csus4 C Csus4 C
us.
earth.
earth.
2. We
Build Your

Chorus
G Am F
king - dom here, let the dark - ness

C
G
Am
fear. Show Your might - y ___ hand, heal our
F
G
C
G
streets and land. ___ Set Your Church on
Am
F
C
fire, win this na - tion back. Change the
G
Am
F
at - mos - phere, build Your king - dom
G
C
G7sus4
C
G7sus4
here, ___ we pray.
To Coda
C
G7sus4
C
D.S. al Coda
(take 2nd ending)
3. Un -
Coda
C

Forever
(We Sing Hallelujah)

Words and Music by Brian Johnson, Christa Black Gifford, Gabriel Wilson, Jenn Johnson, Joel Taylor and Kari Jobe

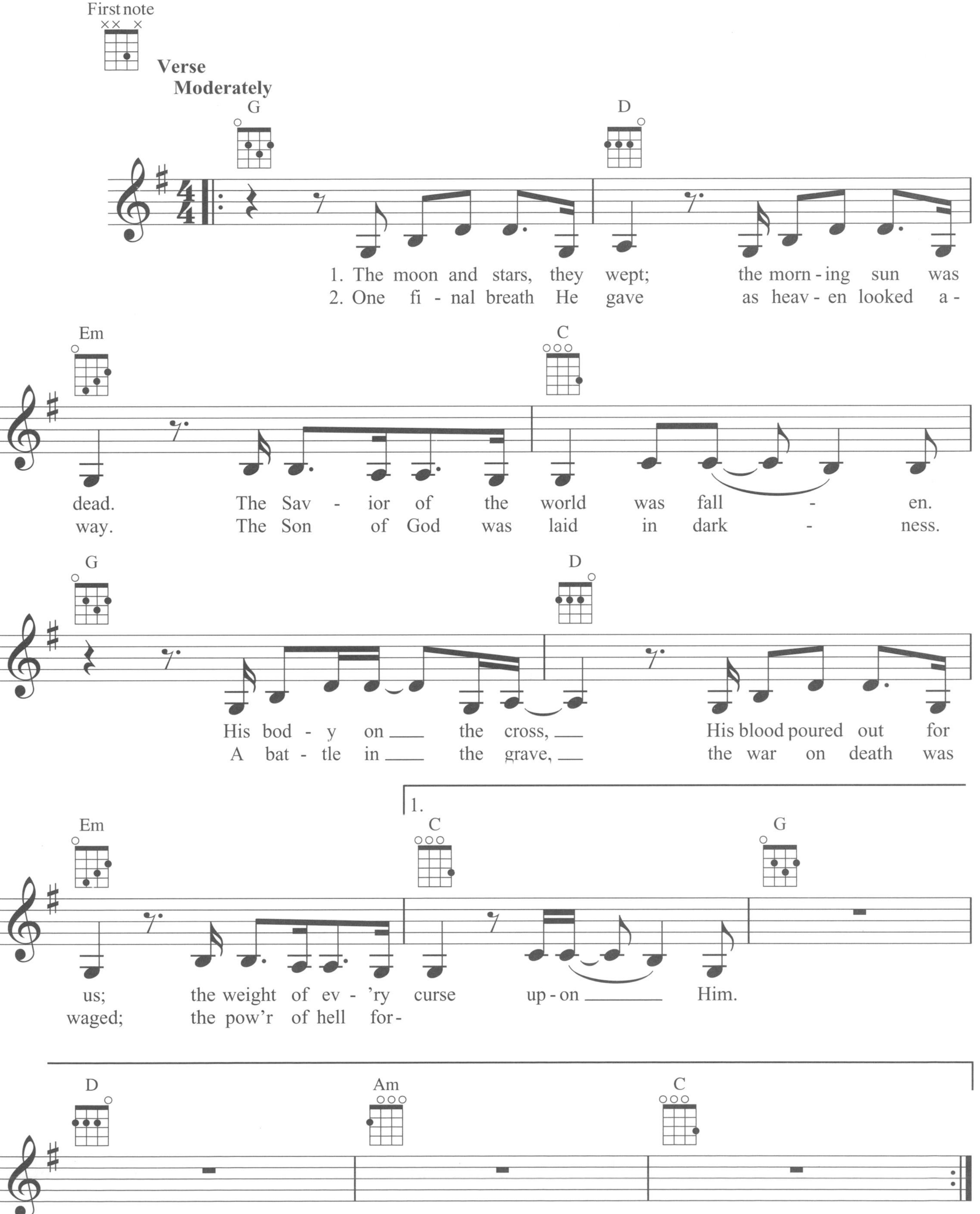

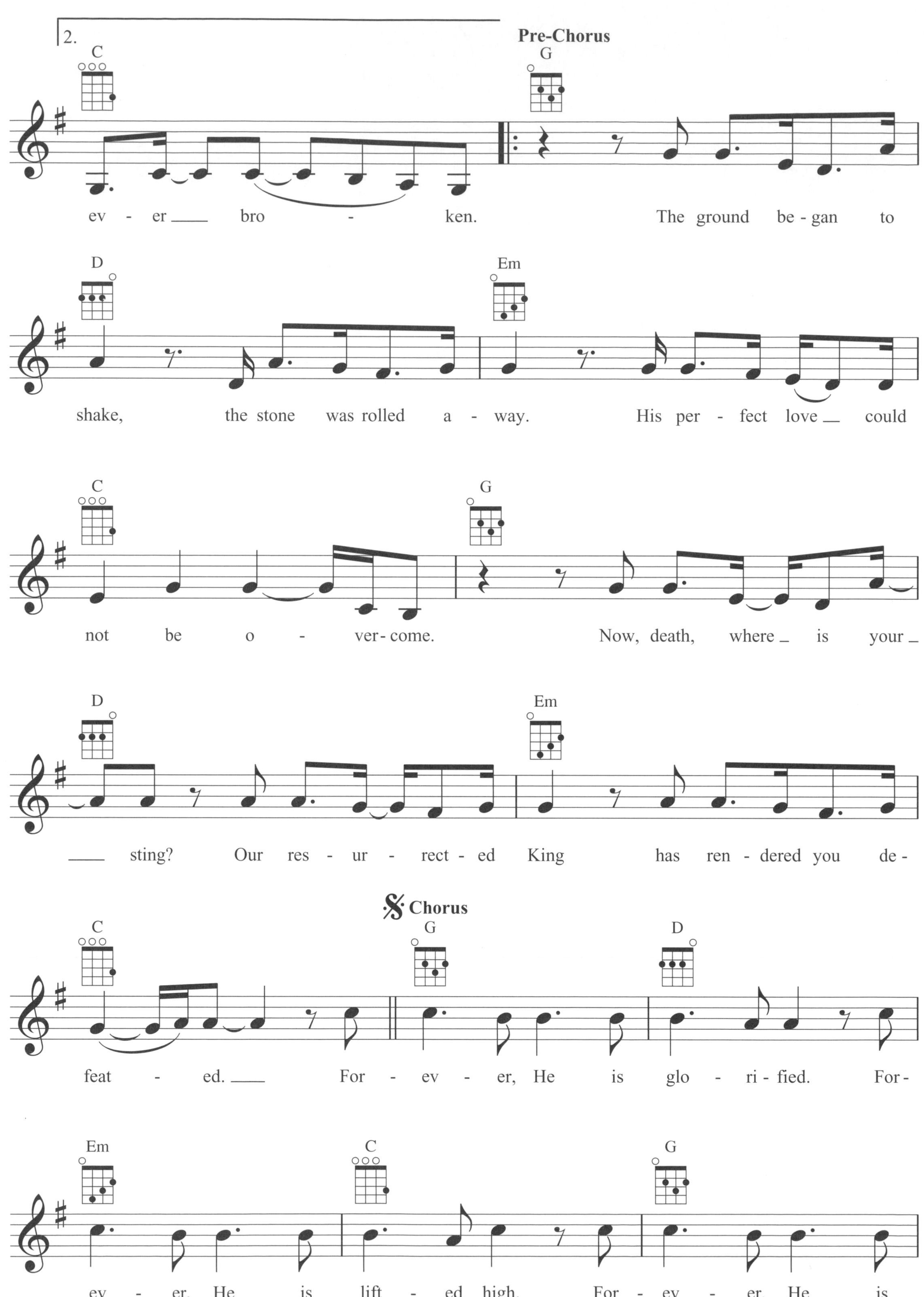

2.
Pre-Chorus
C
G
ev - er bro - ken.
The ground be - gan to
D
Em
shake, the stone was rolled a - way.
His per - fect love could
C
G
not be o - ver - come.
Now, death, where is your
D
Em
sting? Our res - ur - rect - ed King
has ren - dered you de -
Chorus
C
G
D
feat - ed.
For - ev - er, He is glo - ri - fied.
For -
Em
C
G
ev - er, He is lift - ed high.
For - ev - er, He is

To Coda
D
Em
C
ris - en. He is a - live, He is a - live.
Bridge
G
D
We sing hal - le - lu - jah. We sing hal - le - lu -
Em
C
- jah. We sing hal - le - lu - jah, the Lamb has o - ver - come.
G
D
We sing hal - le - lu - jah. We sing hal - le -
Am
C
D.S. al Coda
lu - jah. We sing hal - le - lu - jah, the Lamb has o - ver - come. For-
Coda
Em
C
G
He is a - live.

Ever Be

Words and Music by Kalley Heiligenthal,
Gabriel Wilson, Chris Greely and Bobby Strand

A
Em7
You pledge Your-self to me, and it's why I sing: Your
and known by her true name. And it's why I sing:
Chorus
G
D
Bm
praise will ev-er be on my lips, ev-er be on my lips. Your praise will ev-er be on my
A
G
D
lips, ev-er be on my lips. Your praise will ev-er be on my lips, ev-er be on my lips. Your
Bm
To Coda
1.
A
D
Bm
praise will ev-er be on my lips, ev-er be on my lips.
F♯m
G
2.
A
Bridge
D
lips, ev-er be on my lips.
You will be praised,
A
Bm
G
You will be praised.
With an-gels and saints, we sing, "Wor-thy are You, Lord."
D
D.S. al Coda
And it's why I sing: Your
Coda
A
D
lips, ev-er be on my lips.

Good Good Father

Words and Music by Pat Barrett and Anthony Brown

Am7
D
C
it's who You are, and I'm loved by You. It's who I am,
G
Am7
To Coda 1
To Coda 2
Dsus4
it's who I am, it's who I am.
Verse
D
G
Gsus4
G
2. Oh, and I've seen many searching for answers far and wide. But I know
Gsus4
G
we're all searching for answers only You provide. 'Cause You know
C
G
Am7
just what we need before we say a
D
D.S. al Coda 1
word. You're a good, good Fa-
Coda 1
D
Because You are

Bridge
C
Em7
Am7
per-fect in all of Your ways. Youare per-fect in all of Your ways.
G
C
Em7
Dsus4
You are per-fect in all of Your ways to us.
1.
D
2.
D
Verse
G
Gsus4
G
You are 3. Oh, it's love so un-de-ni-a-ble,
Gsus4
G
Gsus4
G
I, I can hard-ly speak. Peace so un-ex-plain-a-ble,
Gsus4
G
C
G
I, I can hard-ly think as You call me deep-er still, as Youcall
Am7
G
C
G
me deep-er still, as You call me deep-er still in-to love,
Am7
D
D.S. al Coda 2
love, love. You're a good, good Fa-
Coda 2
D
G

Give Thanks

Words and Music by Henry Smith

Great Are You Lord

Words and Music by Jason Ingram, David Leonard and Leslie Jordan

1.
Bb Dm C Csus4 C
on - ly.
2. You give
2.
F
Bridge
F
All the earth will shout Your praise. Our
Dm Bb
hearts will cry, these bones will sing, "Great are You,
1.
F
2.
F
Chorus
Bb
Lord!"
Lord!"
It's Your breath in our
Dm C Bb
lungs, so we pour out our praise, we pour out our praise. It's Your breath in our
Dm C
1.
2.
Bb
lungs, so we pour out our praise to You on - ly. It's Your on - ly.

Holy Spirit

Words and Music by Katie Torwalt and Bryan Torwalt

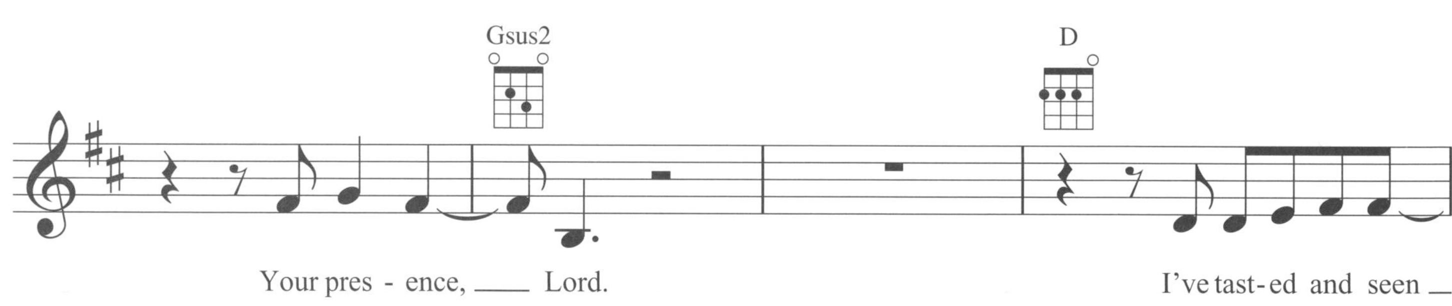

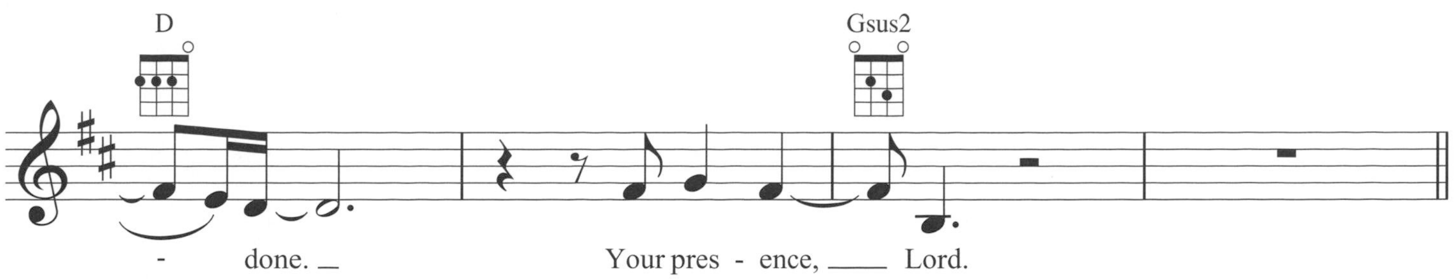
D
Gsus2
- done.
Your pres - ence, Lord.

Chorus

D
G
Ho - ly Spir - it, You are wel - come here. Come flood this place and fill the

Em7
D
at - mos - phere. Your glo - ry, God, is what our hearts long for, to be

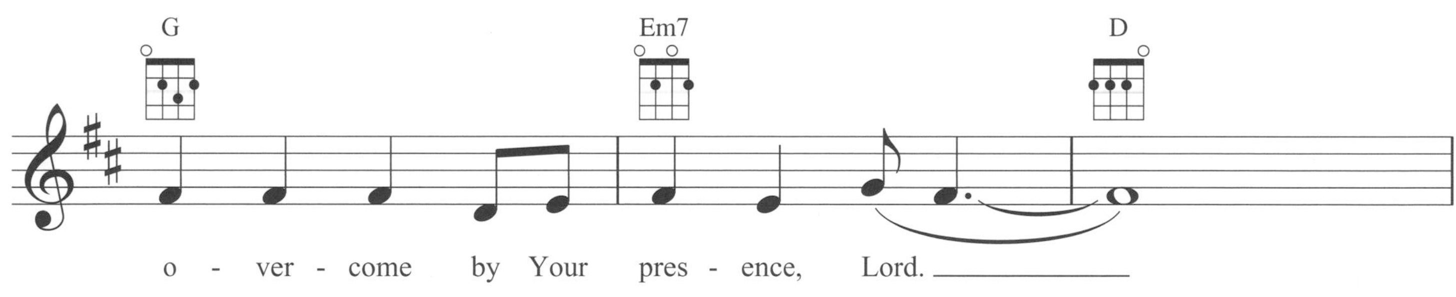
G
Em7
D
o - ver - come by Your pres - ence, Lord.

G
Em7
Your pres - ence, Lord.

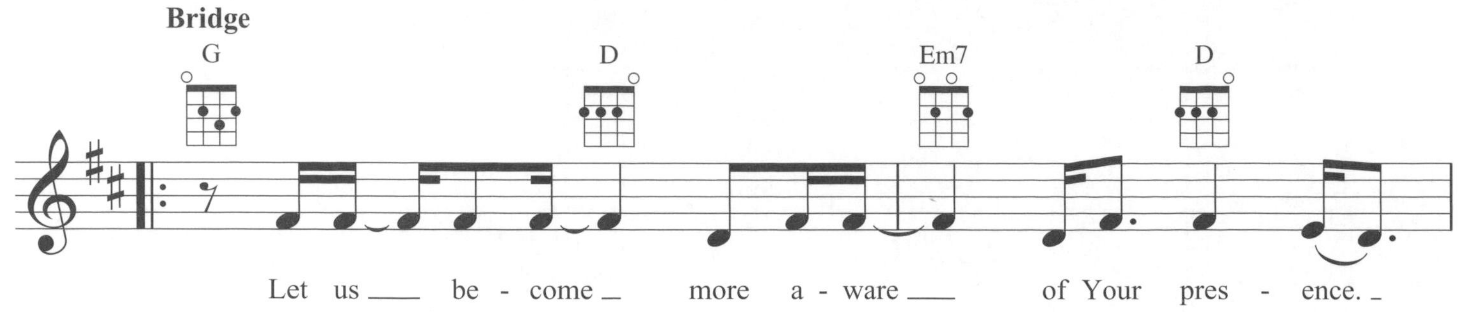
Bridge
G
D
Em7
D
Let us be - come more a - ware of Your pres - ence.

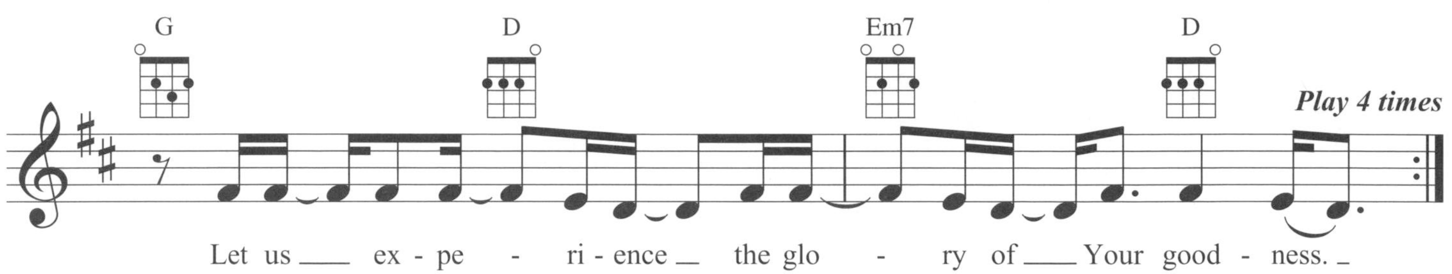
G
D
Em7
D
Play 4 times
Let us ex - pe - ri - ence the glo - ry of Your good - ness.

Outro-Chorus
Gsus2
D
Ho - ly Spir - it, You are wel - come here. Come

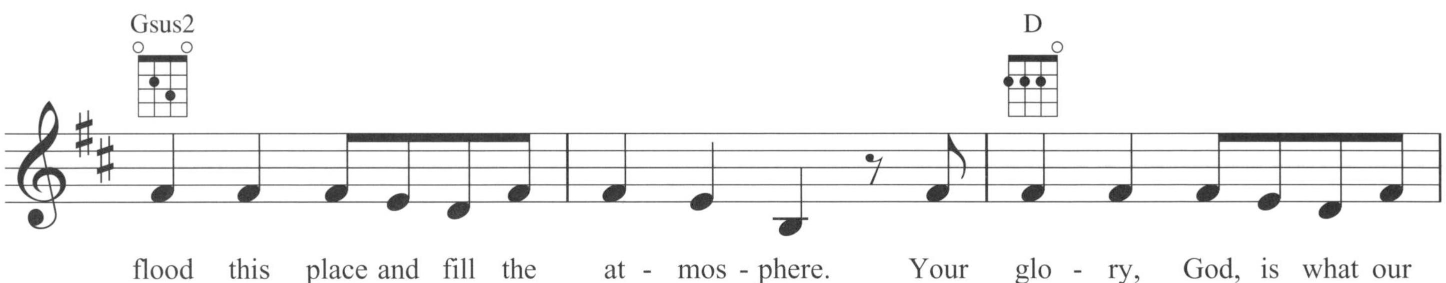
Gsus2
D
flood this place and fill the at - mos - phere. Your glo - ry, God, is what our

Gsus2
Em7
D
rit.
hearts long for, to be o - ver - come by Your pres - ence, Lord.

The Lion and the Lamb

Words and Music by Brenton Brown, Brian Johnson and Leeland Mooring

Bm
A
- dah. He's roar - ing with pow - er and fight - ing our bat -

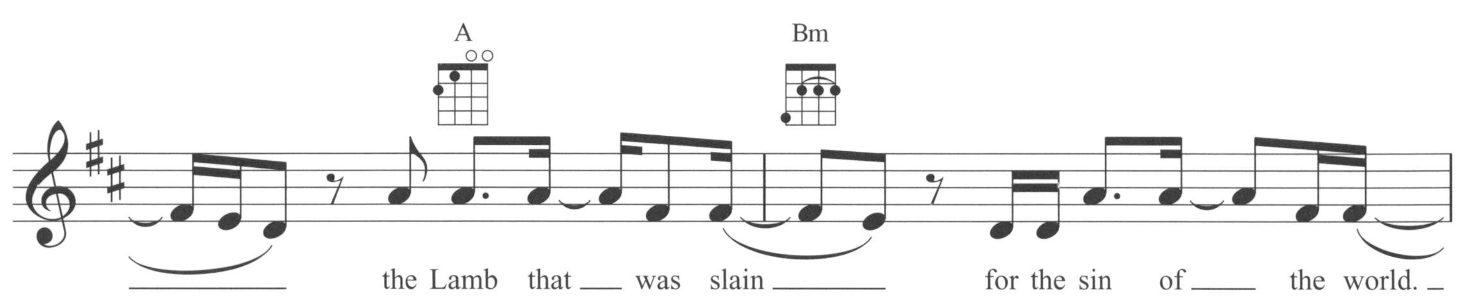
G
A
D
- tles. And ev - 'ry knee will bow be - fore Him. Our God is the Lamb,

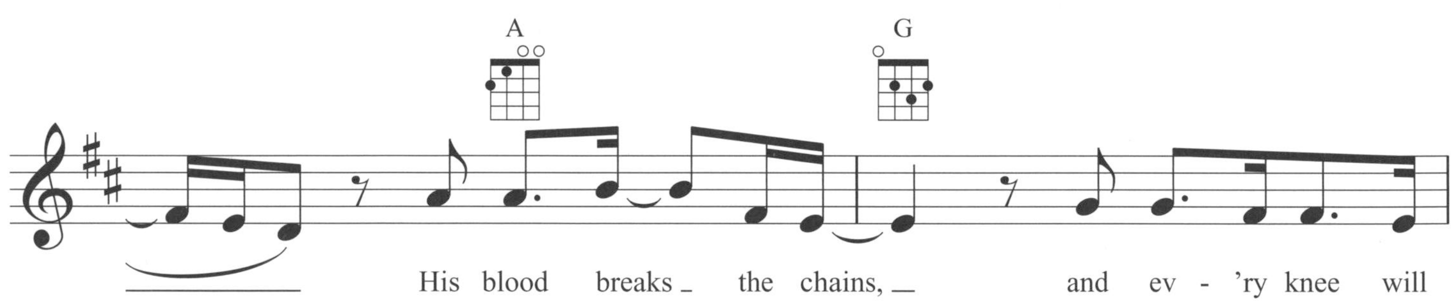
A
Bm
the Lamb that was slain for the sin of the world.

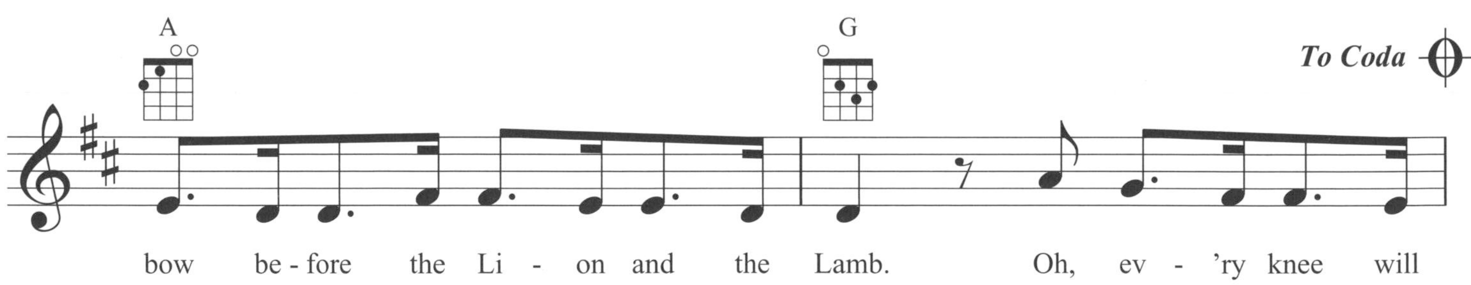
A
G
His blood breaks the chains, and ev - 'ry knee will

A
G
To Coda
bow be - fore the Li - on and the Lamb. Oh, ev - 'ry knee will
A
D
Em
bow be - fore the Li - on and the Lamb.
(Oh, oh.)

1.
2.
Bridge
G
Em
2. So
Who can stop the
D
G
A
Lord Al - might - y? Who can stop the Lord Al - might - y?
Em
D
G
Oh, who can stop the Lord Al - might - y? Who can stop the
A
D.S. al Coda
Coda
Lord?
bow be-fore the Li - on and the
Outro
D
Em
G
Lamb. And ev - 'ry knee will
(Oh, oh.)
1.
2.
D
bow be-fore the Li - on and the bow be-fore the Li - on and the Lamb.

King of My Heart

Words and Music by John Mark McMillan and Sarah McMillan

First note

Verse
Moderately slow

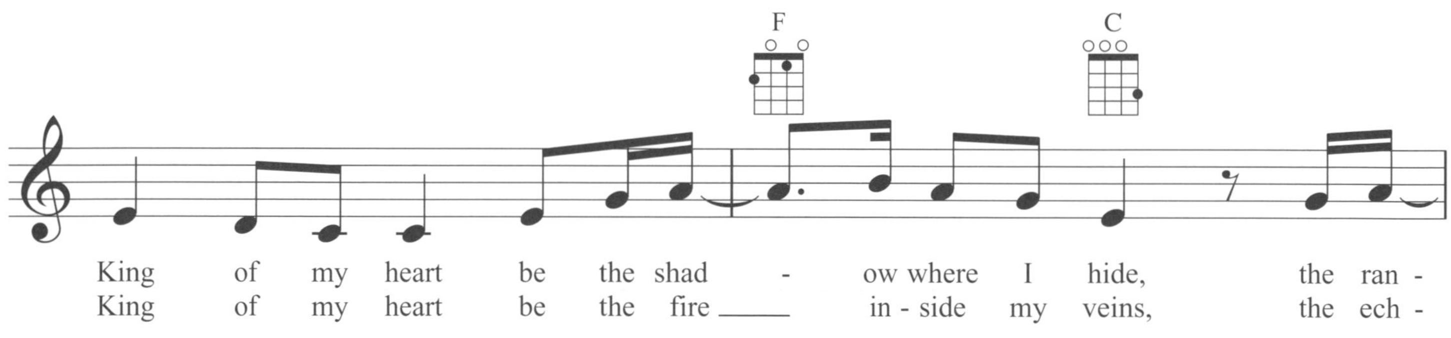

Chorus
Am
C
F
C
Am
C
good, good, oh. You are good, good,
F
C
Am
C
F
C
oh. You are good, good, oh. You are
1.
2.
Am
C
F
C
F
C
good, good, oh. 2. Let the oh.
Bridge
C
You're nev - er gon - na let, nev - er gon - na let me down.
Am
You're nev - er gon - na let, nev - er gon - na let me down.
C
You're nev - er gon - na let, nev - er gon - na let me down.

Am
C
You're nev - er gon - na let, nev - er gon - na let me down.
Bridge
C
F
Gsus4
You're nev - er gon - na let, nev - er gon - na let me down.
Am
C
1. F
Gsus4
You're nev - er gon - na let, nev - er gon - na let me down.
2. F
Gsus4
nev-er gon-na let me down. You are
Chorus
Am
C
F
C
good, good, oh. You are
Am
C
1. F
C
2. F
C
good, good, oh. You are oh.
Bridge
Am
C
F
C
You're nev - er gon - na let, nev - er gon - na let me down.

Am
C
1.
F
C
You're nev - er gon - na let, nev - er gon - na let me down.
2.
F
C
Interlude
Am
G
F
C
nev - er gon - na let me down.
Dm
C
F
Outro
Am
C
When the night is hold - ing on
F
C
Dm
C
F
to me, God is hold - ing on. When the
Am
C
F
C
night is hold - ing on to me,
Dm
C
F
C
God is hold - ing on.

Lead Me to the Cross

Words and Music by Brooke Ligertwood

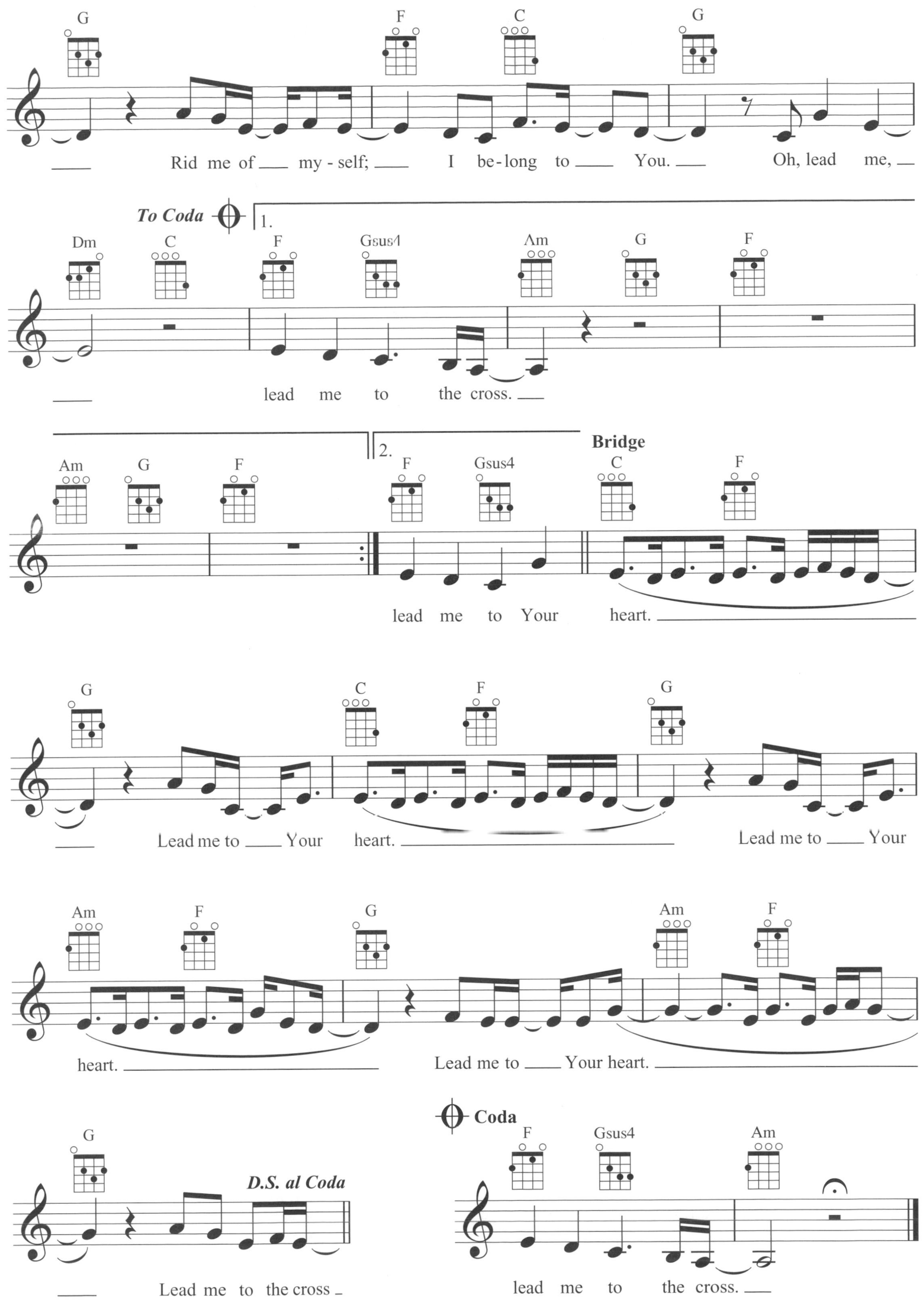
G F C G
Rid me of my-self; I be-long to You. Oh, lead me,
To Coda 1.
Dm C F Gsus4 Am G F
lead me to the cross.
Am G F 2. F Gsus4
Bridge
C F
lead me to Your heart.
G C F G
Lead me to Your heart. Lead me to Your
Am F G Am F
heart. Lead me to Your heart.
G
D.S. al Coda
Lead me to the cross
Coda
F Gsus4 Am
lead me to the cross.

Lord, I Need You

Words and Music by Jessie Reeves, Kristian Stanfill,
Matt Maher, Christy Nockels and Daniel Carson

To Coda
1.
C
G
C
F
God, how I need You.
2. Where sin runs
2.
C
Bridge
F
C
G
Am
You. So teach my song to rise to You
F
G
F
C
G
when temp - ta - tion comes my way. When I can - not stand, I'll fall on
Am
F
G
C
F
D.S. al Coda
You. Je - sus, You're my hope and stay. Lord, I
Coda
C
Outro
C
F
C
F
You. You're my one de - fense, my right - eous - ness. Oh,
C
G
C
C
F
God, how I need You. My one de - fense, my
C
F
C
G
C
right - eous - ness; oh, God, how I need You.

No Longer Slaves

Words and Music by Jonathan David Helser, Brian Johnson and Joel Case

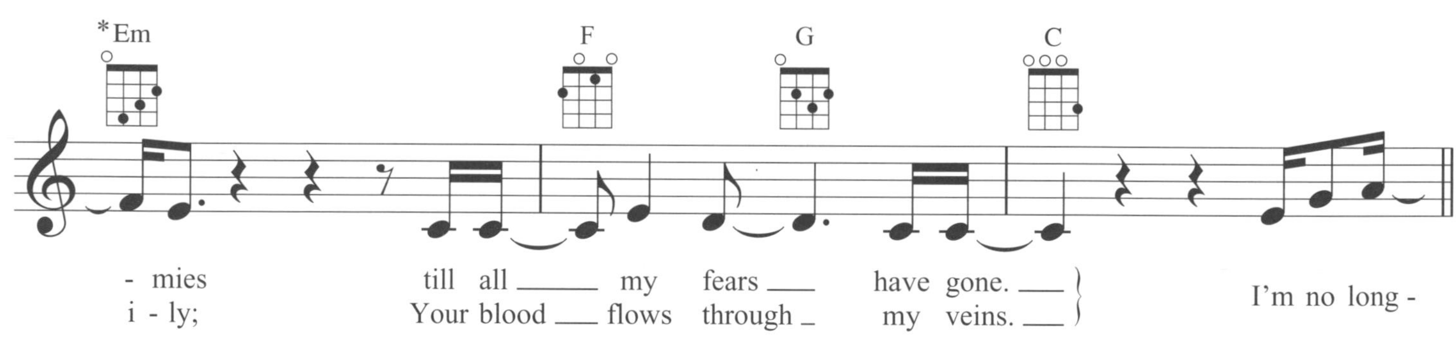

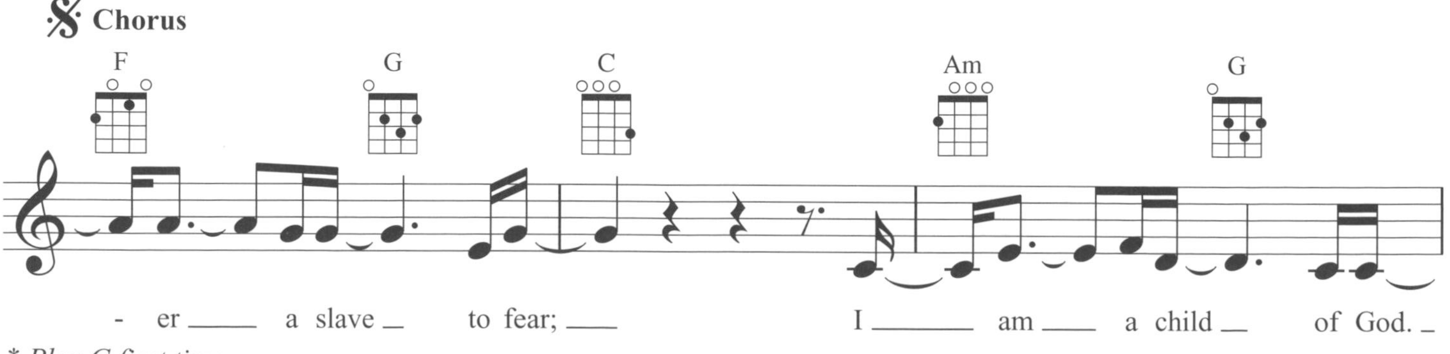

* *Play C first time.*

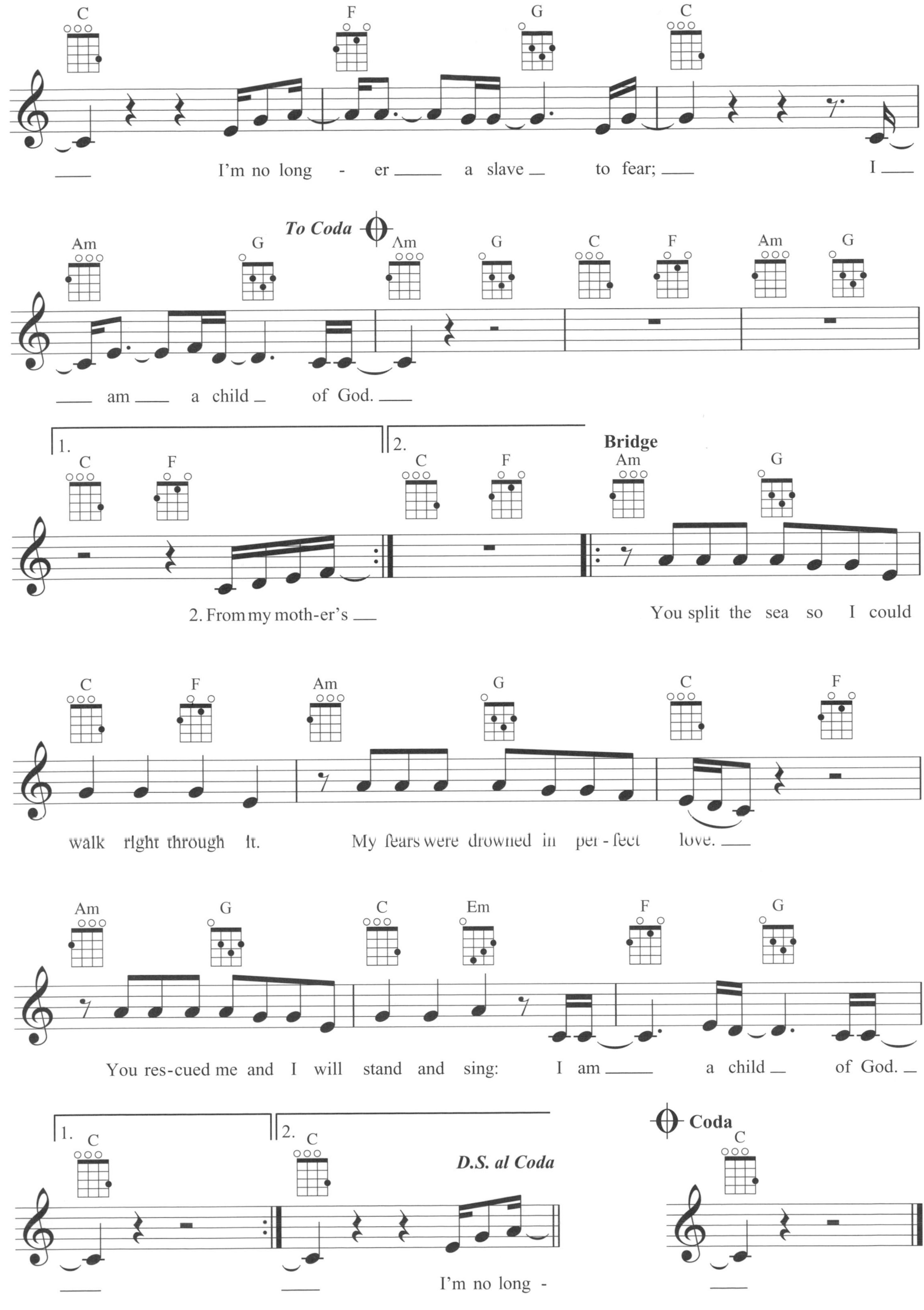
C F G C
I'm no long - er a slave to fear; I
To Coda
Am G Am G C F Am G
am a child of God.
1. C F
2. C F
Bridge
Am G
2. From my moth-er's
You split the sea so I could
C F Am G C F
walk right through it. My fears were drowned in per - fect love.
Am G C Em F G
You res-cued me and I will stand and sing: I am a child of God.
1. C
2. C
D.S. al Coda
I'm no long -
Coda
C

O Come to the Altar

Words and Music by Chris Brown, Mack Brock, Steven Furtick and Wade Joye

Dm Bb F
the Fa - ther's arms are o - pen wide. For - give - ness
Gm7 Dm Bb
was bought with the pre - cious blood of Je - sus Christ.
1.
F Bb F Bb
2., 3.
Chorus
F Gm7 Dm
O come to the al - tar; the Fa - ther's
Bb F Gm7
arms are o - pen wide. For - give - ness was bought with
To Coda
Dm Bb F
the pre - cious blood of Je - sus Christ.

Dm
B♭
O what a
Bridge
F
Dm
Sav - ior; is - n't He won - der - ful?
fore Him, for He is Lord of all.
Sing al - le -
B♭
F
1.
lu - ia, Christ is ris - en.
Bow down be
2.
D.S. al Coda
(take 2nd ending)
Coda
F
Gm7
Dm
Outro
B♭
F
B♭
Bear your cross as you wait for the crown.
F
E♭
B♭
F
Tell the world of the treas - ure you've found.
B♭
F
B♭
F

Oceans
(Where Feet May Fail)

Words and Music by Joel Houston, Matt Crocker and Salomon Lighthelm

First note

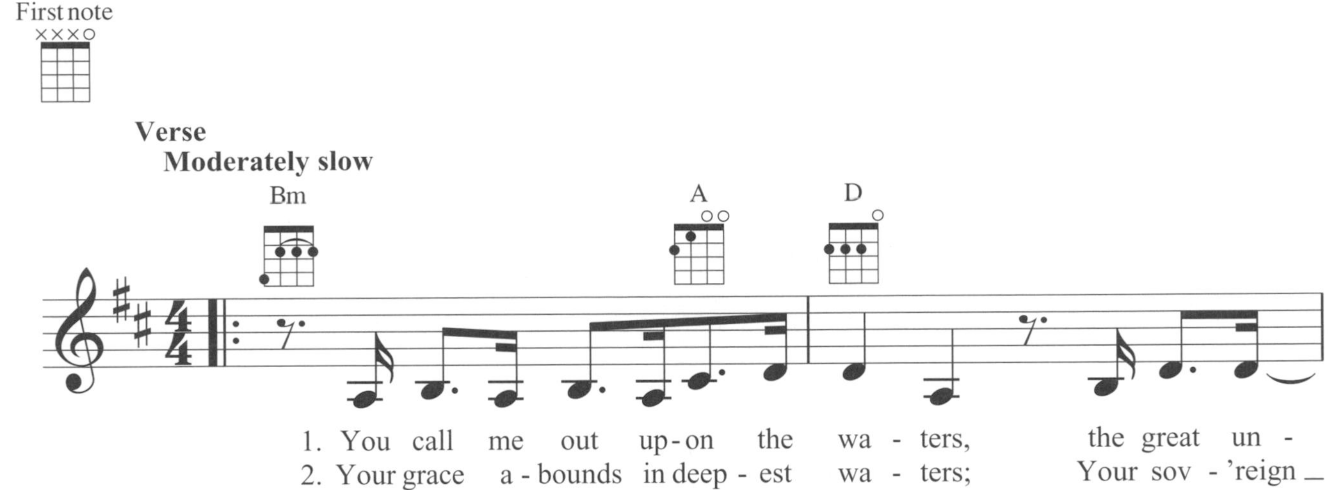

Chorus
G
D
A
And I will call up - on Your name
G
D
A
and keep my eyes a - bove the waves. When o - ceans
G
D
A
rise, my soul will rest in Your em - brace, for I am
G
A
Bm
A
D
Yours and You are mine.
A
G
Bridge
Bm
Spir- it, lead me where my trust
G
D
is with - out bor - ders. Let me walk up-on the wa - ters, wher- ev -

A
Bm
- er You would call me. Take me deep - er than my feet
G
D
could ev - er wan - der, and my faith will be made strong - er in the pres -
Chorus
A
G
D
- ence of my Sav - ior. I will call up - on Your
A
G
D
name. Keep my eyes a - bove the
A
G
D
waves. My soul will rest in Your em -
A
G
A
Bm
- brace. I am Yours and You are mine.

O Praise the Name

(Anástasis)

Words and Music by Marty Sampson, Benjamin Hastings and Dean Ussher

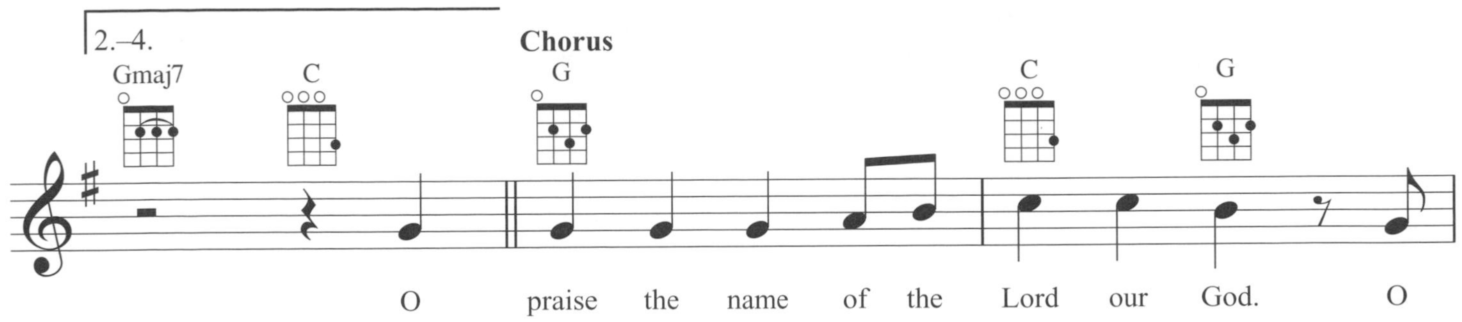
2.–4.
Chorus
Gmaj7
C
G
C
G
O praise the name of the Lord our God. O

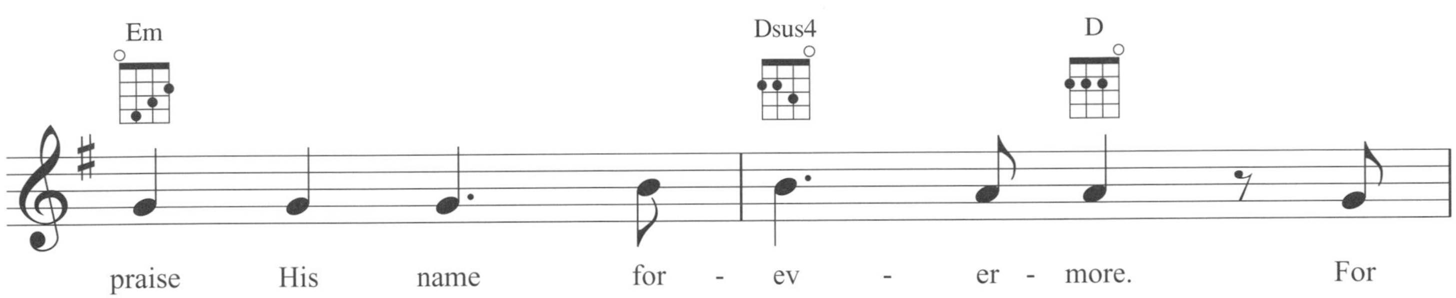
Em
Dsus4
D
praise His name for - ev - er - more. For

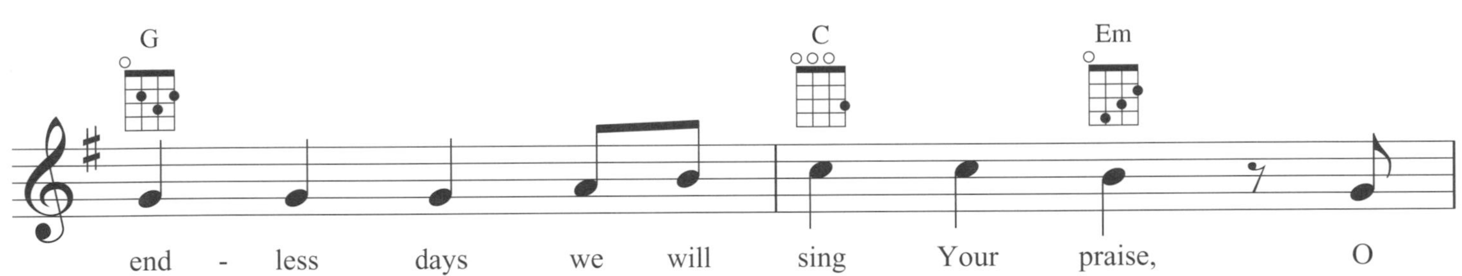
G
C
Em
end - less days we will sing Your praise, O

To Coda
1st time, D.S.
2nd time, D.S. al Coda
(take 2nd ending)
C
Dsus4
D
G
Bm7
C
Lord, O Lord our God.
3. Then on the
4. He shall re -

Coda
Em
C
Dsus4
D
G
God. O Lord, O Lord our God.

Shout to the Lord

Words and Music by Darlene Zschech

Chorus
B♭ Gm E♭ F
Shout to the Lord, all the earth, let us sing
B♭ Gm E♭ F
pow - er and maj - es - ty, praise to the King.
Gm E♭ F E♭
Moun-tains bow down and the seas will roar at the sound of Your
F B♭ Gm E♭ F
name. I sing for joy at the work of Your hand. For-
B♭ Gm E♭ F Gm
ev - er I'll love You, for - ev - er I'll stand. Noth-ing com-pares to the prom -
E♭ F B♭ F B♭
1. 2.
- ise I have in You.

This I Believe
(The Creed)

Words and Music by Ben Fielding and Matt Crocker

F
Gm
B♭
C
I be - lieve in the res - ur - rec - tion,
that we will rise a - gain,
Dm
B♭
C
1.
B♭
Dm
for I be - lieve in the name of Je - sus.
C
F
B♭
Dm
C
F
2.
F
I be -
Bridge
B♭
Dm
C
F
- lieve in You.
I be -
B♭
Dm
C
F
B♭
- lieve You rose a - gain.
I be - lieve that Je -
C
F
1.
2.
- sus Christ is Lord.
I be -

Chorus
F
Gm
B♭
C
(1., 2., 4.) I be - lieve in God our Fa - ther, I be - lieve in Christ the Son,
(3.) I be - lieve in life e - ter - nal, I be - lieve in the vir - gin birth.

Dm
B♭
I be - lieve in the Ho - ly Spir - it. Our God is Three in One.
I be - lieve in the saints' com - mun - ion and in Your ho - ly Church.

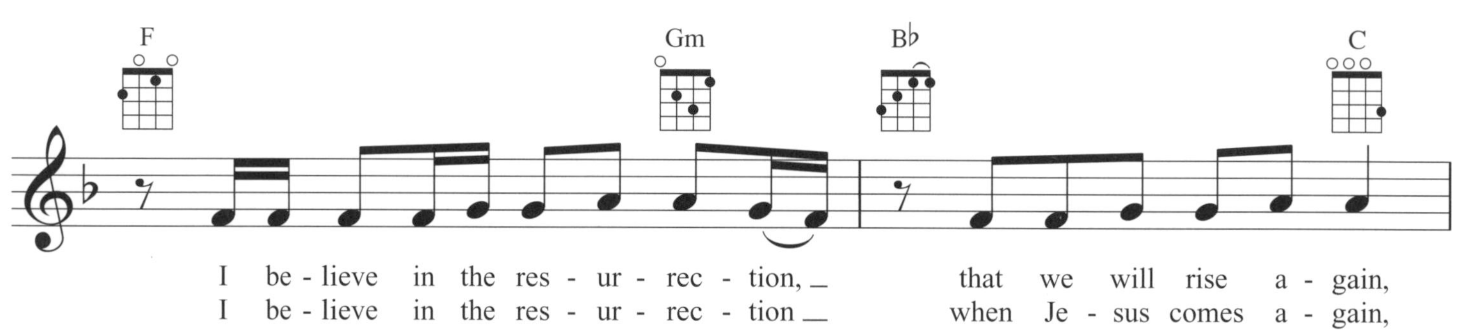
F
Gm
B♭
C
I be - lieve in the res - ur - rec - tion, that we will rise a - gain,
I be - lieve in the res - ur - rec - tion when Je - sus comes a - gain,

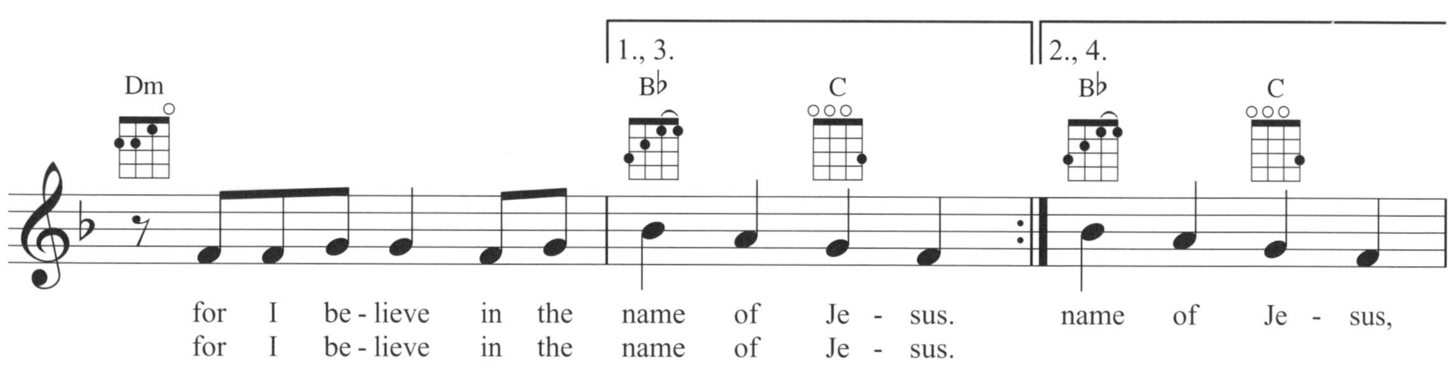
1., 3.
2., 4.
Dm
B♭
C
B♭
C
for I be - lieve in the name of Je - sus. name of Je - sus,
for I be - lieve in the name of Je - sus.

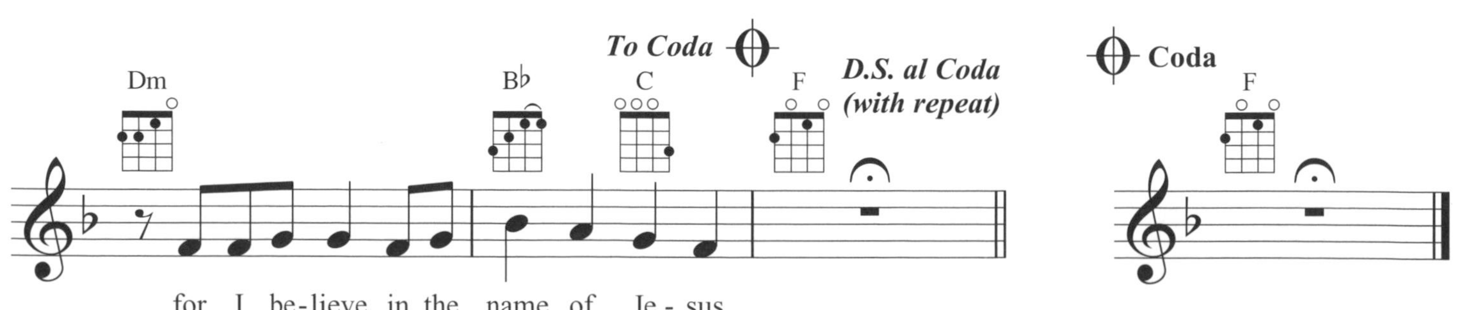
To Coda
D.S. al Coda (with repeat)
Coda
Dm
B♭
C
F
F
for I be - lieve in the name of Je - sus.

You Are My All in All

By Dennis Jernigan

Note: The Verse and Chorus may be sung simultaneously.

This Is Amazing Grace

Words and Music by Phil Wickham, Joshua Neil Farro and Jeremy Riddle

F
Am
and leaves us breath - less in awe and won - der?
shines like the sun in all of its bril - liance?
The King of glo - ry,
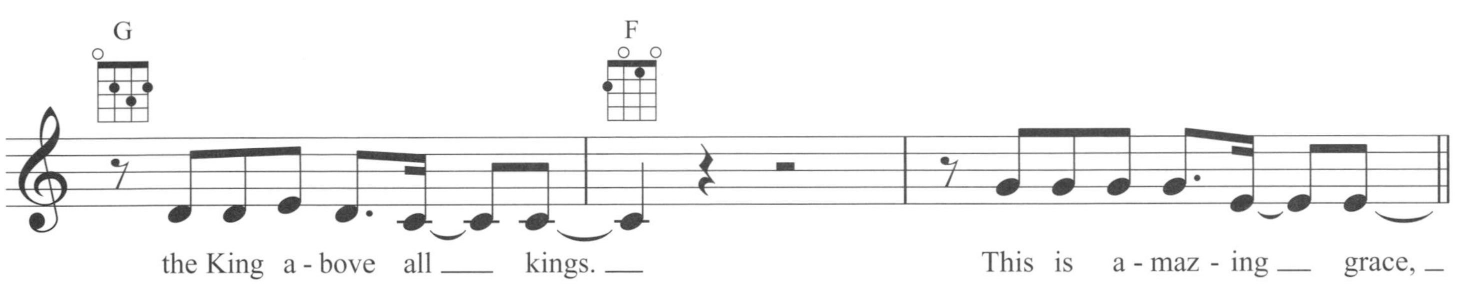
G
F
the King a - bove all kings.
This is a - maz - ing grace,

Chorus
C
F
this is un - fail - ing love,
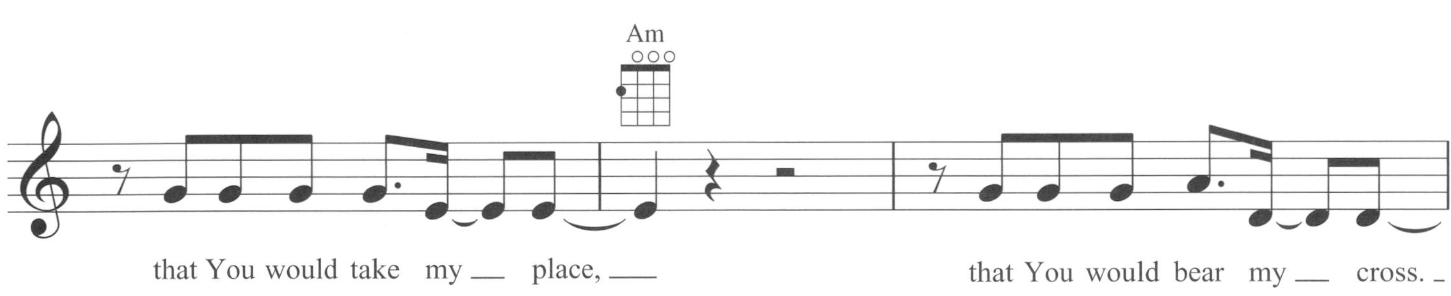
Am
that You would take my place,
that You would bear my cross.

G
C
You laid down Your life

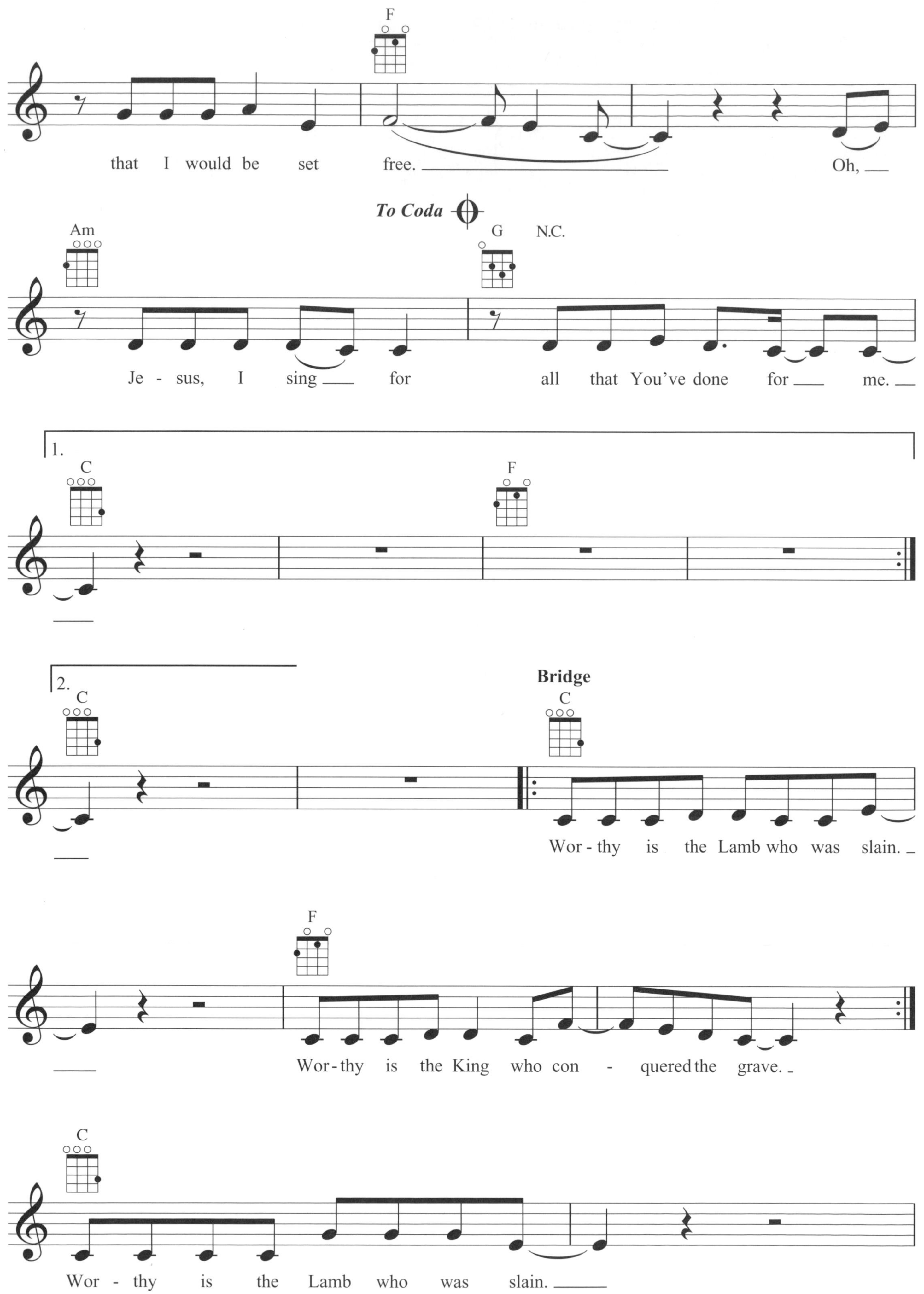
F
that I would be set free.
Oh,
To Coda
Am
G
N.C.
Je - sus, I sing for all that You've done for me.
1.
C
F
2.
C
Bridge
C
Wor - thy is the Lamb who was slain.
F
Wor - thy is the King who con - quered the grave.
C
Wor - thy is the Lamb who was slain.

F
Wor - thy is the King who con - quered the grave.

Am
C
Wor - thy is the Lamb who was slain. Wor - thy, wor -

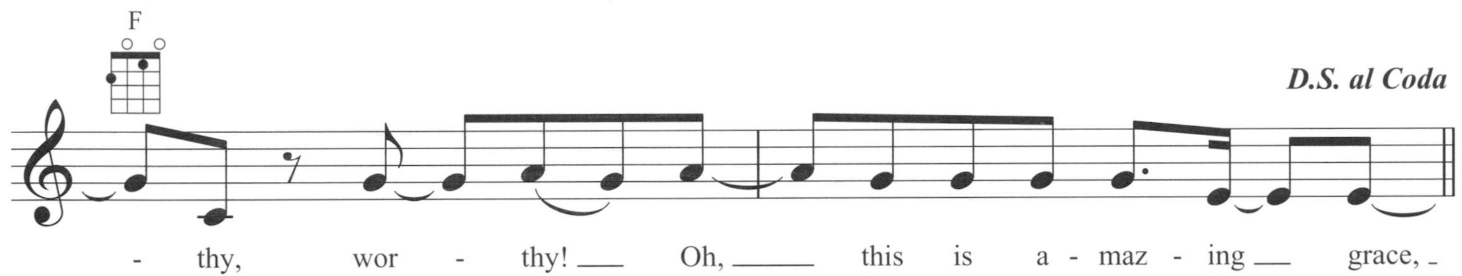
F
D.S. al Coda
- thy, wor - thy! Oh, this is a - maz - ing grace,

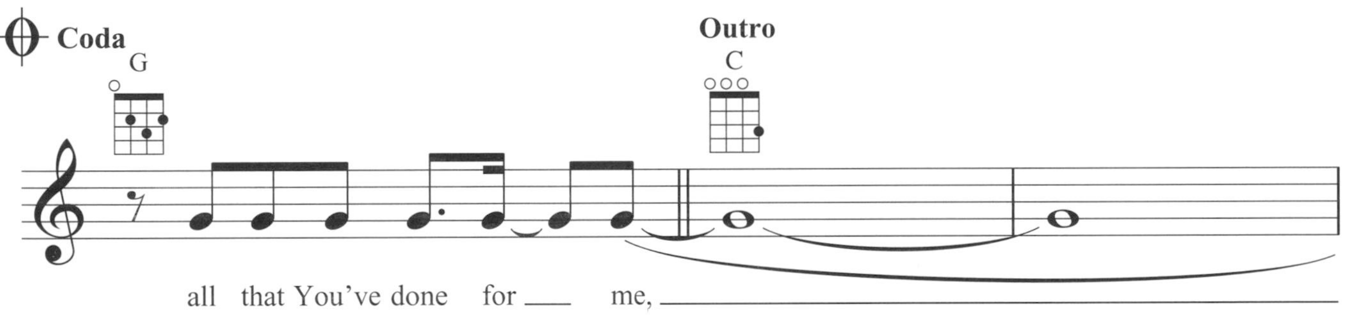
Coda
Outro
G
C
all that You've done for me,

F
C
all that You've done for me.

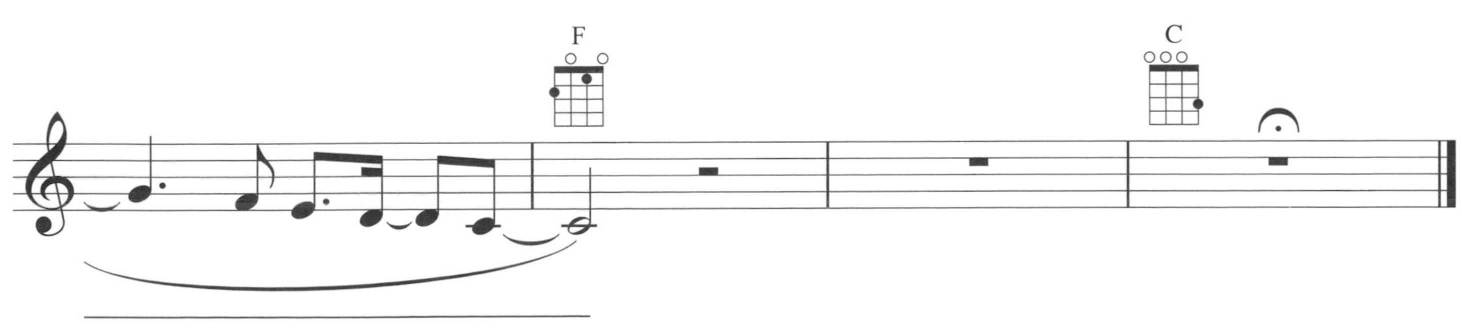
F
C

Your Name

Words and Music by Paul Baloche and Glenn Packiam

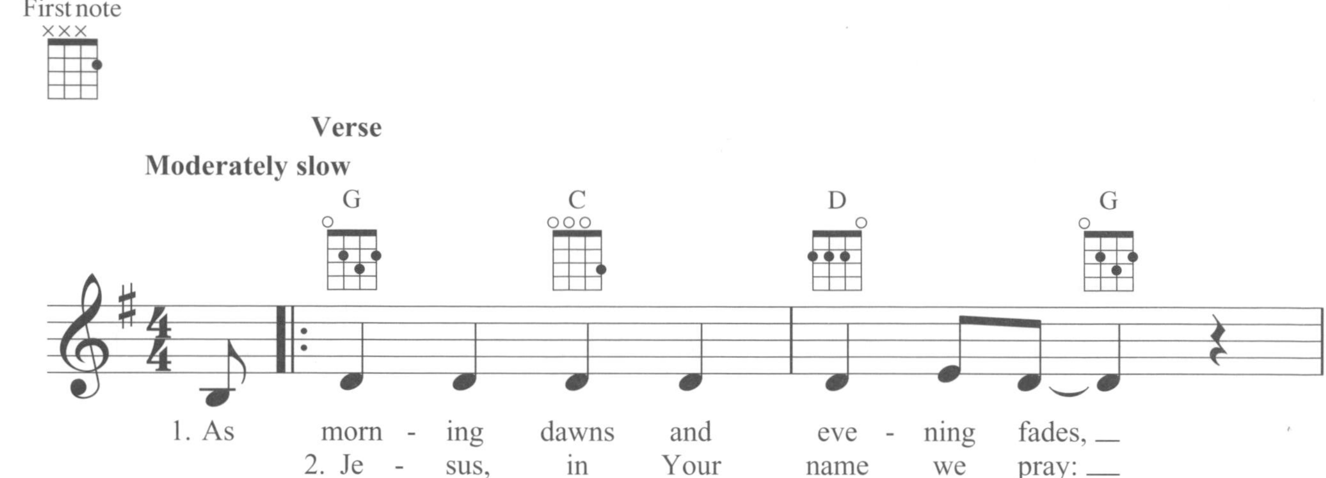

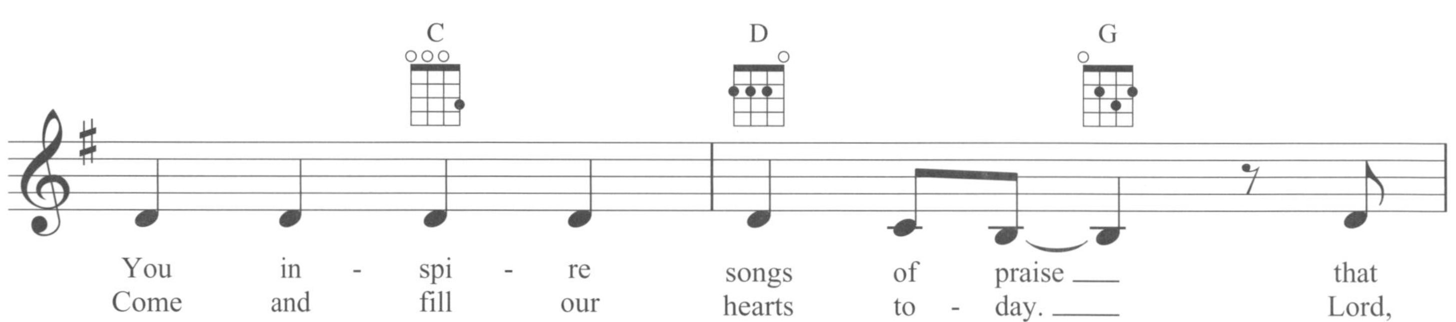

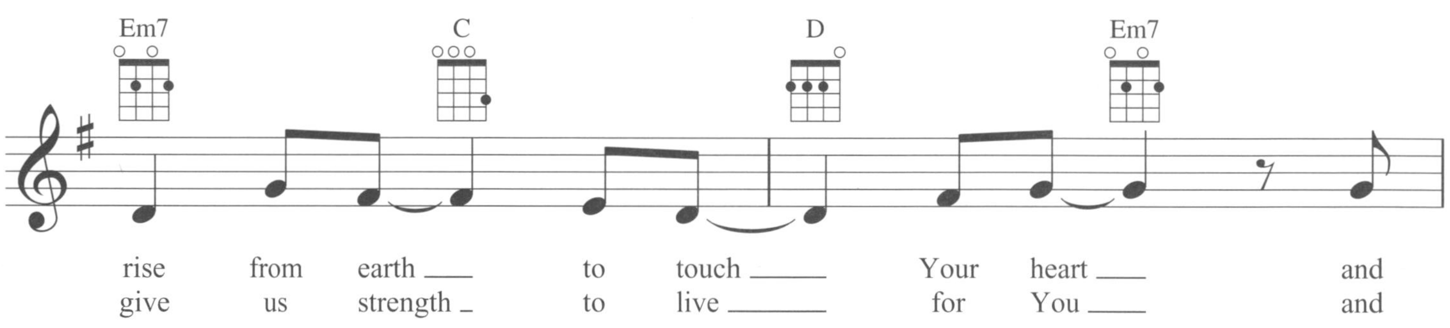

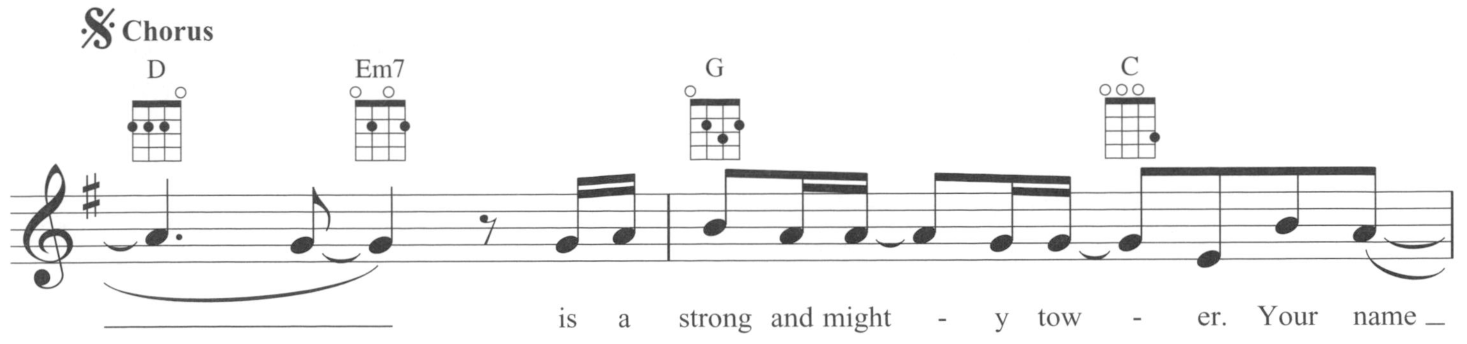
Chorus
D
Em7
G
C
is a strong and might - y tow - er. Your name

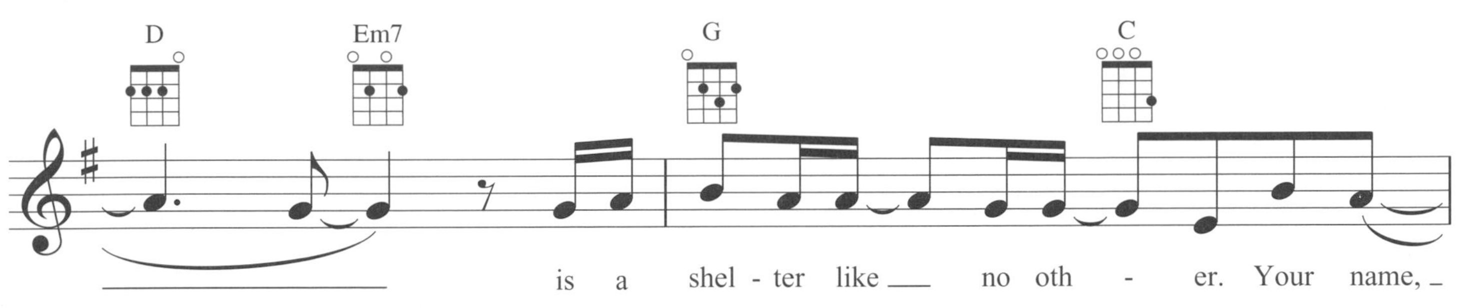
D
Em7
G
C
is a shel - ter like no oth - er. Your name,

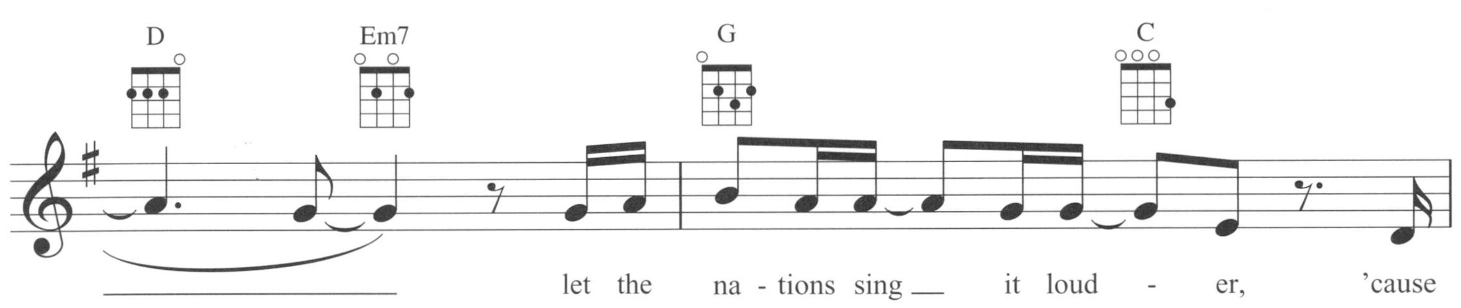
D
Em7
G
C
let the na - tions sing it loud - er, 'cause

G
C
D
To Coda
1.
G
C
noth-ing has the pow - er to save but Your name.

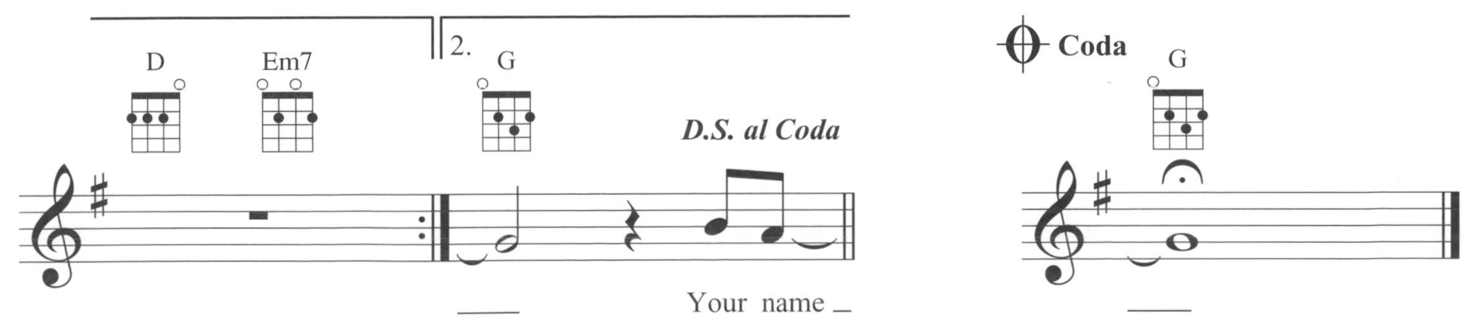
D
Em7
2.
G
D.S. al Coda
Your name
Coda
G

What a Beautiful Name

Words and Music by Ben Fielding and Brooke Ligertwood

Bm
A
G
- sus Christ, my King. What a beau-ti-ful name it is,
- sus Christ, my King. What a won-der-ful name it is,
- sus Christ, my King. What a pow-er-ful name it is,
D
A
noth-ing com-pares to this. What a beau-ti-ful name it is,
noth-ing com-pares to this. What a won-der-ful name it is,
noth-ing can stand a-gainst. What a pow-er-ful name it is,
To Coda
1.
Bm
A
G
the name of Je - sus.
the name of Je -
the name of Je -
2.
G
Interlude
G
A
- sus.
(Instrumental)
1., 2.
3.
Bm
F♯m
A
Death could not hold

Bridge
G
A
You, the veil tore be - fore You. You si - lence the boast
- val, You have no e - qual. Now and for - ev -
Bm
F♯m
of sin and grave. The heav - ens are roar -
- er, God, You reign. Yours is the king -
G
A
Bm
- ing the praise of Your glo - ry, for You are raised to life a - gain.
- dom, Yours is the glo - ry, Yours is the name a - bove all names.
1.
A
You have no ri -
2.
A
D.S. al Coda
What a pow - er - ful name it is,
Coda
G
Outro
Bm
A
- sus. What a pow - er - ful name it is, the name of Je -
G
Bm
A
G
- sus. What a pow - er - ful name it is, the name of Je - sus.

PREFACE

This set of three anthems by Maurice Greene (1696–1755), published by the Church Music Society to mark the 75th anniversary of its inauguration in 1906, has been newly edited from the original collection of *Forty Select Anthems*, which appeared in London in 1743. The subsequent, revised editions of ?1745 and 1770 have also been consulted.

Abbreviations in the source text have been amplified, misprints rectified, and punctuation rendered consistent, without further reference. The commentary below draws attention to instances of unclear or ambiguous underlay. Editorial slurs are shown thus:

Original note-values have been retained and also – except where noted below – original barring. The interpretation of appoggiaturas notated as grace-notes is specified, in all cases, in the commentary. Note-groupings have been made regular, superfluous accidentals omitted, and *fermata* added where these are not included in the source.

All editorial matter is printed in small type or within square brackets. The ranges of the respective voice-parts are indicated at the beginning of each movement, as are suggested metronome markings – intended only as an approximate guide. 'Solo' has been substituted for Greene's designation 'verse', and 'full' for 'chorus', in the vocal parts.

The notation of the continuo figuring follows present-day practice. Figures in italics are supplied from the editions of ?1745 and 1770.

The realization of the continuo bass for organ (manuals only) is editorial. In the interests of preserving line and texture in the keyboard writing, a harmony note referred to by the figures may occasionally be missing from the organ continuo if it is already present in a voice-part or if the harmonic sense is sufficiently explicit without it. Also, one or two vocal appoggiaturas are doubled or otherwise accommodated in the continuo part, although figures are lacking.

I should like to thank Watkins Shaw and David Rowland for kindly helping in the preparation of this edition.

April 1981

Richard Marlow
Cambridge

COMMENTARY

1 O GOD OF MY RIGHTEOUSNESS

ANTHEM for 2 Voices. PSALM IV.

Text Largo Andante: verse 1
Adagio-Andante-Adagio: verses 2 & 3 (parts only)
Largo Andante: verse 9
Andante: verses 5 & 4 (part only)

2.org: since the G appears as a semiquaver, double dotting may be intended during this movement. The opening bars of each part, in this alternative reading, are indicated by editorial rhythm-signs above the staves / 11.org.beat 2: figures $^{6}_{5}$ / 14.org.beat 1: figures $^{5}_{3}$ / 60.ten & 62.sop & ten: elision of syllables editorial / 98, 112 & 114.sop.beat 2: D (or G) appoggiaturas added to coincide with continuo harmony, following Greene's cadential practice elsewhere / 120.org.beat 1: figuring $^{7}_{\flat}$ (♭ misplaced) / 130.org: figuring aligned with quaver F, 7♮ (♮ misplaced) / 134.org: figuring aligned with 2nd quaver F, $^{6}_{4}$ / 141–2.org: figuring included but inaccurately aligned in 1743.

Appoggiaturas printed as grace-notes in the source have been interpreted as follows:

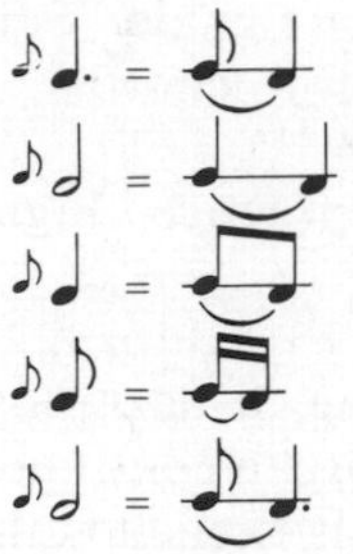

bars 6, 12, 20, 32, 38, 42, 46, 55, 57, 86
bar 8
bars, 74, 76, 78, 92, 93, 95, 102, 103
bar 104 (twice)
bar 153
105.sop.1st quaver beat:

2 BLESSED ARE THOSE THAT ARE UNDEFILED IN THE WAY

ANTHEM for two Voices. PSALM CXIX. 1st Part.

Text Largo: verses 1 & 2
Recitative: verse 4
Andante: verses 5 & 18
Vivace: verses 15 & 16
Vivace: verses 171 & 172

In the Andante movement the composer may well have intended the rhythm  to be interpreted in a more relaxed manner as  , particularly in juxtaposition with the triplet-quaver sequences.

114.sop2: no B appoggiatura / 168.ten & 171.bass: underlay slurs confused / 174.sop2: no D appoggiatura / 183.ten & bass: underlay unclear / 185.org: 'verse' brought forward from the beginning of bar 186.

Appoggiaturas printed as grace-notes in the source have been interpreted as follows:

bars 3, 6, 38, 114, 116, 134, 136, 138

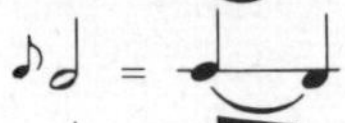

bars 17, 22, 24, 56, 72, 82, 88, 130, 132, 152, 164, 174, 184, 191, 197, 201, 210, 216, 232, 234

bars 24, 39, 55, 62

bar 227.alto

3 LET MY COMPLAINT COME BEFORE THEE, O LORD

FULL ANTHEM for 5 Voices. Psalm CXIX, last Part.

Text Largo: verses 169 & 170
Andante: verses 171 & 172

All time-signatures are editorial / 8.org: figure 7 aligned with minim G / 17–18: one bar only in source / 25.org.3rd minim beat: figures $\frac{6}{4}$ / 42.alto: slur misplaced over previous C–B♮ pair / 43–44.ten & 47–48.sop2: slur over B♭–C crotchets only /54.sop2: E♭ for D / 59.2nd minim beat – 60.1st minim beat.org: right-hand part a 3rd too low / 65–67: editorial barring. At 65 Greene has a bar of two minims' duration, followed by two bars of four minims' worth. He inserts another bar lasting two minims half-way through 67 to restore the $\frac{4}{2}$ sequence thereafter / 69 & 71.bass: minims G–C slurred.

Appoggiaturas printed as grace-notes in the source have been interpreted as follows:

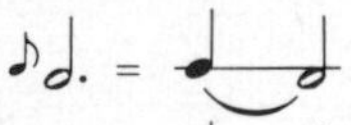

bar 25

bars 30, 70, 72

1. O GOD OF MY RIGHTEOUSNESS

Verse anthem for soprano and tenor soloists, S.A.T.B. chorus, and organ continuo

MAURICE GREENE
Forty Select Anthems, London, 1743,
Volume Two, *pp* 79–84
Edited by Richard Marlow

Verses from Psalm IV

*See commentary, p. iv

Printed in Great Britain

20
tr
— me when I call, — hear me, hear me when- I
tr
call, when I call, — hear — me, hear — me, hear — me when- I
20
9 6 6 4 5 3 6 9 6 6 5 7 6 4 5 3♮
25
call; hear — me, hear — me, O
tr
call; O God of my — righ - teous-ness, hear me when I call, —
25
6 6 9 8 5 6 4 3
30
tr
God of my — righ - teous-ness, hear me when I call; hear — me — when I
hear — me — when I call, hear —
30
6 5 6♮ 5 4 3 5 4 3 5

35
call, hear — me when I call. Thou hast set me — at —
— me, hear — me when I call.
tr
9 8 7 6 4 5 3 6 6 5 6 4 5 3 6 6♮
40
li - ber - ty when I was in trou - ble, in trou - ble,
Thou hast set me — at — li - ber - ty
6 ♮ 6 6 ♮
45
when — I was in trou - ble, in trou - ble, when — I was, —
when I was in trou - ble, in trou - ble, in trou - ble, when I was, —
7 ♮ 6 ♭ 7 ♮ ♭ 6 5 ♮

50
— I was— in trou - ble, have mer - cy up - on — me, have
— I was— in trou - ble, have mer - cy up - on — me, have
55
mer - cy, have mer - cy, have mer - cy, have mer - cy up - on me,
mer - cy, have mer - cy, have mer - cy, have mer - cy, have mer - cy— up - on me,
60
and hear - ken un - to my prayer,
and hear - ken un - to my prayer, hear - ken un - to my prayer,

65
hear - ken un-to my prayer, hear - ken un-to — my prayer, hear - - ken,
hear - ken un-to my prayer, hear - ken un-to — my prayer, hear - ken,
70
hear - ken un-to — my prayer.
hear - ken un-to — my prayer.
Adagio [♩ = c 66]
SOLO
TENOR
75
O ye sons of men, how long, — how long will ye blas-pheme mine
Andante [♩ = c 72]
ho - nour, how long will ye blas-pheme mine ho - nour, and have plea - sure in va - ni - ty?

80
Adagio [♩ = c 66]
have plea - sure in va - ni - ty? Know___ this; the Lord hath cho - sen to him -
85
- self the man that is god - ly, the Lord hath cho - sen to him - self_ the man that is god - ly.
Largo Andante [♩ = c 52]
90
SOPRANO
SOLO
I will lay_ me_ down in_ peace, will lay_ me_ down in_ peace, will lay_ me_ down in_

peace, will lay me down in peace, and take my rest: for it is thou, 'tis thou, O

Lord, that mak'st me to dwell, to dwell in safe-ty, to dwell in safe-ty, to dwell in safe-ty;

I will lay me down in peace, will lay me down in

peace, will lay me down in peace, and take my rest, and take my rest:

for it is thou, 'tis thou, O Lord, that mak'st me to dwell in safe-ty, for it is

110
thou, 'tis thou, O Lord, 'tis thou, O Lord, that mak'st me to dwell in safe-ty, that mak'st
me to dwell in safe - ty, to dwell in safe-ty, to dwell in safe-ty, mak'st me to dwell in safe - ty.
115
Andante [𝅗𝅥 = c 48]
SOPRANO
ALTO
TENOR
BASS
FULL
And put your trust in the Lord,
FULL
And put your trust in the
FULL
Of - fer the sac - ri - fice of righ - teous - ness,
115
Andante [𝅗𝅥 = c 48]

120
and put your trust in the Lord,
and put your trust in the
Lord, your trust in the Lord, in the Lord,
and put your
and put your trust in the Lord.
FULL
Of - fer the sac - ri - fice of righ - teous - ness,
Lord,
and put your trust in the Lord,
and put your trust in the
trust in the Lord, and put your trust in the Lord,
and put your trust in the
Stand in awe, and
Stand in awe, and sin not,

125
Lord; Of - fer the sac - ri - fice of righ - teous-
Lord, put your trust in the Lord, the Lord, and put your
sin not, put your trust in the Lord;
Of - fer the sac - ri - fice of righ - teous - ness,
125
ness, and put your trust, your trust in the Lord,
trust in the Lord, put your trust in the Lord,
Of - fer the sac - ri - fice of righ - teous - ness,
Of - fer the sac - ri - fice of righ - teous-ness,

130
and put your trust in the Lord, and put your trust in the Lord;
stand in awe, and sin not, and put your trust in the Lord,
stand in awe, and sin not,
130
stand in awe, and sin not, stand in awe,
135
and put your trust in the Lord, your trust in the Lord, in the
and put your trust in the Lord, in the Lord, and put your
Of - fer the sac - ri - fice of righ - teous -
135

*This phrase may have to be transferred to the tenor part.

and put your trust in the Lord, and put your
and put your trust in the Lord, and put your trust in the Lord,
and put your trust in the Lord; stand in awe, and sin not,
stand in awe, and sin not,
145
trust in the Lord; Of - fer the sac - ri - fice of righ - teous-
put your trust in the Lord, and put your
and put your trust, your trust in the Lord, put your trust in the
and put your trust in the Lord.
145

150
- ness, and put your trust in the Lord, and put your trust in
trust in the Lord, put your trust, your trust put,
Lord, in the Lord, and put your trust in the Lord,
Of - fer the sac - ri - fice of righ - teous - ness, and
150
the Lord, put your trust, your trust in the Lord.
put your trust in the Lord, your trust in the Lord.
the Lord, put your trust in the Lord.
put your trust in the Lord.

2. BLESSED ARE THOSE THAT ARE UNDEFILED IN THE WAY

Verse anthem for two soprano soloists, S.A.T.B. chorus, and organ continuo

MAURICE GREENE
Forty Select Anthems, London, 1743
Volume Two, *pp* 1–8
Edited by Richard Marlow

Verses from Psalm CXIX

 Printed in Great Britain

tr
15
Lord; Bles - sed are they that keep his tes - ti - mo - nies, and
tr
Lord; Bles - sed are they that keep his tes - ti - mo - nies, and seek
15
7 6♯ 4 3 4 3 4 3 6 4 5 3♯ 6
tr
seek him with their whole heart.
tr
Bles - sed are they that keep
him with their whole heart. Bles - sed are they that keep, that
tr
6♮ 5 6 5 6 4 ♯ 6 6 4 5 4 3
20
tr
his tes - ti - mo - nies, and seek him with their whole heart, and seek him
[tr]
keep his tes - ti - mo - nies, and seek him with their whole heart, and seek
20
4 3 7 6 5 4 3 9 8 7 6 4 5 3 7♮ 9 8

tr
25
with— their— whole— heart.
tr
— him with their whole— heart.
25
7 6 4 5 3 6 6 5 6 6 5 6 4 5 3
Recitative [♩ = c 63]
SOLO
SOPRANO
30
Thou hast charg- ed that we shall di - li-gent- ly keep thy com - mand - ments,
6 ♯
Thou hast charg - ed that we shall di - li-gent - ly keep thy com - mand - ments.
6 6♮ 6 5♮ 6 4 5 3
35 Andante [♩ = c 88]
SOLO
SOPRANO
O that my ways were made so— di - rect,— that I might
6 6 6 7

* See commentary, p. iv

65
tr
sta - tutes; O - pen thou mine eyes, o - pen thou mine eyes, that I may
70
see the won - - - - - - drous things of thy law; o - pen thou mine
tr
75
eyes, o - pen thou mine eyes, that I may see the won - - - -
80
- - - - - - - drous things of thy law; that I may see, that I may
85
see the won - - - - - - drous, the won-drous things of thy law.
tr

90
Vivace [♩ = c 92]
SOPRANO I
SOPRANO II
SOLO
Then will I talk, will I talk of thy com-mand-ments and
have res - pect un - to thy ways.
Then will I
talk, will I talk of thy com - mand-ments and have res - pect un - to thy
SOLO
Then will I talk, will I talk of thy com -
mand-ments, and have res - pect, and have res - pect un-to thy
95
tr

100
ways. Then will I talk of thy com - mand - ments, and
ways. Then will I talk of thy com - mand - ments, and have res - pect, and
100
have res - pect un - to thy ways, and have res - pect un - to thy ways.
105
have res - pect un - to thy ways, and have res - pect un - to thy ways.
105
My de - light shall be in thy sta -
My de - light shall be in thy sta - tutes, my de -

110
-tutes, my de-light_ shall_ be, shall be in thy
-light_ shall_ be in thy___ sta-tutes, thy sta - - -
110
115
sta-tutes, and I will not, I will not for-get___ thy word, I
-tutes, I will not for-get___ thy word, and I will not, I
115
will not for-get___ thy word. Then will I
will not for-get___ thy word. Then will I talk, will I talk of thy com-

120
talk, will I talk of thy com - mand-ments, and have_ res - pect un-to thy
- mand-ments, and have res - pect, and have_ res - pect_ un - to thy
120
ways, and have res - pect un - to thy ways. My de - light shall be in thy_
ways, and have res - pect un-to thy ways.
125
___ sta-tutes, my de - light shall be, my de - light shall be, shall
My de-light shall be in thy sta - tutes, my de-light shall be, my de - light shall

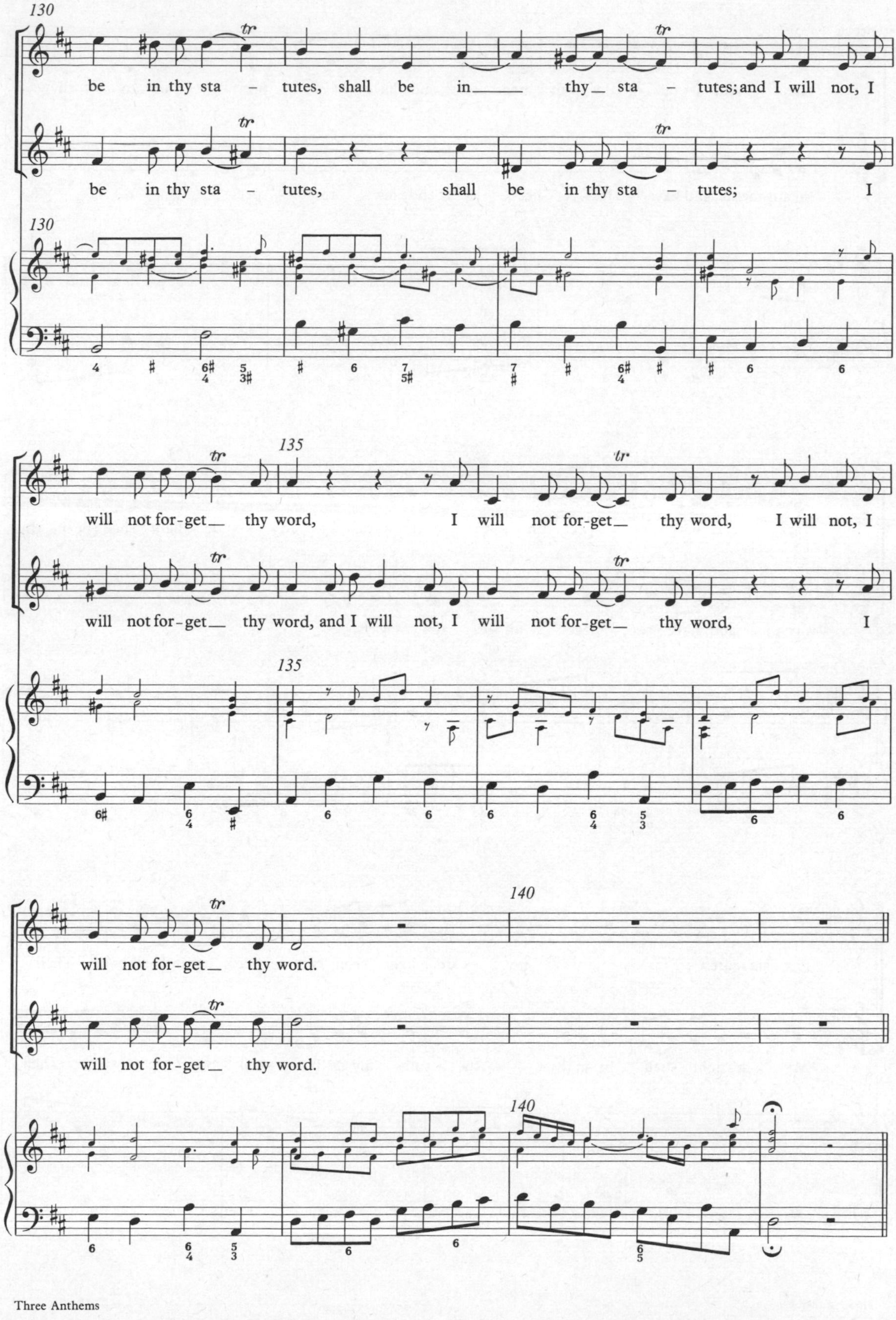

130

be in thy sta – tutes, shall be in___ thy_ sta – tutes; and I will not, I

be in thy sta – tutes, shall be in thy sta – tutes; I

135

will not for-get_ thy word, I will not for-get_ thy word, I will not, I

will not for-get_ thy word, and I will not, I will not for-get_ thy word, I

140

will not for-get_ thy word.

will not for-get_ thy word.

Vivace [♩ = c 120]
145
SOPRANO I
SOPRANO II
ALTO
TENOR
BASS
SOLO
My lips shall
VERSE
150
when thou hast taught me, hast taught me thy sta -
speak of thy praise, hast taught me thy sta -
155
- tutes. My lips shall
- tutes. My lips shall speak of thy praise,
tr

* Solo range

160
speak of thy praise, hast taught me thy sta -
when thou hast taught me, hast taught me thy sta -
165
170
- tutes. FULL Yea, my
- tutes. FULL Yea, my
FULL Yea, my tongue shall sing of thy word, shall sing of thy word, yea, my
FULL Yea, my tongue shall sing, shall sing of thy word,
FULL Yea, my tongue shall
CHORUS

SOLO
175
tongue shall sing of — thy — word, of — thy — word; for all thy com-mandments are
SOLO
tongue shall sing of — thy — word, of — thy — word; for all thy com-mandments are
tongue shall sing, shall sing of thy word;
yea, — my — tongue shall sing of — thy — word;
sing, shall sing, shall sing of — thy — word;
175
VERSE
180
FULL
right-eous, all thy com-mand-ments are right-eous; for all, all thy com -
FULL
right-eous, all thy com-mand-ments are right-eous; for all, all thy com -
FULL
for all, all thy com -
FULL
for all, all thy com -
FULL
for all, all thy com -
180
CHORUS

185
SOLO
mand - ments are righ - teous. My lips shall
SOLO
mand - ments are righ - teous. My lips shall speak of thy praise,
mand - ments are righ - teous.
mand - ments are righ - teous.
mand - ments are righ - teous.
185
VERSE
190
speak of thy praise, My lips shall speak of thy praise,
thy praise, My lips shall
190
195
200
thy praise, when thou hast taught me, hast taught me
speak of thy praise, when thou hast taught me, hast taught me
195
200

FULL
205
thy sta - tutes. Yea, my tongue shall sing, shall sing of thy word;
FULL
thy sta - tutes. Yea, my tongue shall sing, shall sing of thy word;
FULL
Yea, my tongue shall sing of thy word; yea, my
FULL
Yea, my tongue shall sing,
FULL
Yea, my tongue shall sing of thy word;
205
CHORUS
210
yea, my tongue shall sing of thy
yea, my tongue shall sing of thy
tongue shall sing, shall sing of thy word, shall sing of thy word,
yea, my tongue shall sing of thy word, shall sing of thy word, shall
yea, my tongue shall
210

215
SOLO
word, shall sing of thy word; for all thy com -
SOLO
word, shall sing of thy word; for all thy com -
shall sing, shall sing of thy word;
sing, shall sing of thy word, of thy word;
sing, shall sing, shall sing of thy word;
215
VERSE
220
- mand-ments are righ - teous, all thy com - mand-ments are righ - teous; for all,
FULL
- mand-ments are righ - teous, all thy com - mand-ments are righ - teous; for all,
FULL
for all,
FULL
for all,
FULL
for all,
220
CHORUS

225
all thy com - mand-ments are righ - teous; all, all thy com -
all thy com - mand-ments are righ - teous; all, all thy com -
all thy com - mand-ments are righ - teous; all thy com -
all thy com - mand-ments are righ - teous; all thy com -
all thy com - mand-ments are righ - teous; all, all thy com -
230
-mand-ments are righ-teous, are righ - teous, are righ - teous.
-mand-ments are righ-teous, are righ - teous, are righ - teous.
-mand-ments are righ - teous, are righ - teous, are righ - teous.
-mand-ments are righ-teous, are righ - teous, are righ - teous.
-mand-ments are righ - teous, are righ - teous, are righ - teous.
235

3. LET MY COMPLAINT COME BEFORE THEE, O LORD

Full anthem for S.S.A.T.B. chorus and organ continuo

MAURICE GREENE
Forty Select Anthems, London, 1743,
Volume Two, *pp* 25–29
Edited by Richard Marlow

Verses from Psalm CXIX

Printed in Great Britain

Oxford University Press
Walton St., Oxford OX2 6DP

- plaint — come, let my com - plaint
let my com - plaint let my com - plaint —
come be - fore — thee, come be - fore — thee, come be -
- plaint, let my com - plaint — come be - fore — thee,
- plaint come be - fore — thee,
4 3♯ 6 4 3♯ 6 7 4 3♮
10
come be - fore — thee, let my com - plaint
come be - fore — thee, let my com - plaint — come,
- fore — thee, O Lord; let my com -
let my com - plaint come, come be - fore — thee,
let my com - plaint, — let my com -
10
5 4 2 6 4 3♮ 6

15
come be - fore — thee, come — be - fore — thee, come —
let my com - plaint come be - fore — thee, come be -
plaint — come, come be - fore — thee, come be - fore —
let my com - plaint — come — be - -
- plaint come be - fore — thee, come be - fore — thee,
15
— be - fore — thee, O Lord; give me,
- fore — thee, O Lord; give me,
thee, O — Lord; give me, — give me
fore thee, O Lord; give me — un - -
O — Lord; give me

20
give me un - der - stand - ing ac - cor - ding
give me un - der - stand - - ing ac - -
un - der - stand - ing give me un - der - stand - -
der stand - ing, give me un - der - stand - ing
un - der - stand - ing ac -
20
4 3♮ 6 5 2 6 5 7
25
tr
to thy word, ac - - cor - ding to thy word; let
cor - ding to thy word, ac - - cor - ding to thy word; let,
- ding ac - cor - - ding, ac - cor - - ding to thy word; let, let
ac - cor - - ding to thy word;
- cor - ding to thy word, to thy word;
25
2 6 6 4 6 5 5 3 8 6 8 6 2 7 5 2 7 6 4 [5] 4 5 3 ♭

my sup - pli - ca - tion come, come
let my sup - pli - ca - - - - tion
my sup - - - - - pli - ca - tion come
let my sup - pli - - ca - tion
let my sup - pli - ca - tion come be -
30
be - fore thee; de - li - ver me, de - li - ver
come be - fore thee; de - li - ver me, de - li - ver
be - fore thee; de - li - ver me, de - li - ver me,
come be - fore thee; de - li - ver me, de - li - ver
-fore, be - fore thee; de - li - ver me, de - li - ver
30

35
me, de - li - ver me ac - cor - ding to thy word,
me, de - li - ver me ac - cor - ding to thy word,
de - li - ver me, ac - cor - ding
me, de - li - ver me, ac - cor - ding to thy
me, de - li - ver me, ac -
35
40 Andante [𝅗𝅥 = c 88]
to thy word.
ac - cor - ding to thy word.
to thy word.
word, to thy word. My lips shall speak of thy
- cor - ding to thy word. My lips shall speak
40 Andante [𝅗𝅥 = c 88]

when thou hast taught me thy
when thou hast taught me thy sta - -
when thou hast taught me thy sta - - tutes;
praise
thy sta -
of thy praise
when thou hast
3♮ 3♮ 2 4♮ 2
45
sta - - tutes;
when thou hast
- tutes; my lips shall speak of thy praise
thy sta - tutes; my lips shall speak of thy praise
- - tutes; my lips shall speak of thy praise
taught me thy sta - - tutes;
45
6 9 7 6 5 6 5 6 ♮

taught me thy sta - - tutes; my lips shall speak of thy
thy sta - - tutes; my lips shall
when thou hast taught me thy sta - tutes; my lips shall speak
when thou hast taught me thy sta - - tutes; thy sta - tutes;
when thou hast taught me thy sta - tutes;
6
6
50
praise
when thou hast taught me thy
speak of thy praise
when thou hast taught, hast taught
of thy praise
when thou hast taught
when thou hast taught me thy sta - tutes;
when thou hast taught me thy sta - -
50
3♮
6
3♮
2
4♮
2
6
7

55
sta - - tutes; yea, my
me thy sta - tutes; yea, my tongue
me thy sta - tutes; yea, my
thy sta - tutes; yea, my tongue shall sing,
- tutes, thy sta - tutes; yea, my tongue, yea,
55
7 6♮ 5
60
tongue shall sing, shall sing of thy word, shall sing of thy word,
shall sing of thy word, shall sing of thy word,
tongue shall sing, shall sing of thy word, shall sing of thy
shall sing of thy word, shall sing, shall sing of thy
my tongue shall sing of thy word, shall
60
5 6 2 6 5 6
3♭

tr
shall sing of thy word shall sing of thy
shall sing of thy word, shall sing of thy
word, shall sing of thy word;
word, shall sing, shall sing, shall sing of thy
sing, shall sing, shall sing of thy
65
word; for all thy com-mand - ments are
word; for all thy com-mand - ments are righ - teous,
for all thy com - mand - ments are righ - teous, for
word; for all thy com-mand - ments are righ - teous,
word; for all thy com - mand - ments are righ - teous,
65

ISBN 019-395321-8
9 780193 953215

Processed and printed by
Halstan & Co. Ltd., Amersham, Bucks., England